Love Is **Here.**

A Teenager's Call to (Outstretched) Arms.

LOVE IS HERE

Published by The Sowing Room

All rights reserved. No part of this book may be used or reproduced in any form for purposes other than personal use without written permission from the publisher. Brief excerpts may be used for review purposes.

Unless otherwise indicated, all Scripture quotations are taken from the Holy Bible, New Living Translation, copyright 1996, 2004. Used by permission of Tyndale House Publishers, Inc., Wheaton, Illinois 60189. All rights reserved.

Scripture taken from the NEW AMERICAN STANDARD BIBLE®, Copyright © 1960,1962,1963,1968,1971,1972,1973,1975,1977,1995 by The Lockman Foundation. Used by permission.

© 2010 Zach Michel

First Edition 2010

ISBN 978-0-578-06127-6

To Mom

…because you said this was important.

<u>NOTE</u>

I'm not a brilliant author.
I'm not a genius.
I'm only a teenager.
But I am a prince in Christ's Kingdom.
And I'm tired of sitting on my throne.
I'm tired of doing nothing.
I want to do something.
I want to fight.
I want to advance the Kingdom.
I want to step off my throne.
I want to head to the front lines.
And I want to lead an Army of Princes and Princesses into battle.

This is the call.

- Zach Michel

CONTENTS

Intro: Get Real — 7

Part One – The People
I	–	Our Role As Teenagers	13
II	–	Our Battlefield: Today's Culture	19
III	–	Sabotage Of The Heart	27

Part Two – The Passion
IV	–	The Design Of The Heart	35
V	–	The Broken Heart	41
VI	–	The Teenage Heart	45

Part Three – The Problem
VII	–	Carried Away	53
VIII	–	The Teenage "Needs"	59
IX	–	The Opposite Sex	67

Part Four – The Pain
X	–	Seeking The Truth	77
XI	–	Accepting The Truth	85
XII	–	The Truth Has Set Us Free	91

Part Five – The Purpose
XIII	–	Teenagers Are Made To Love…	99
XIV	–	The Foundation For Life	105
XV	–	Get The Picture	113

Part Six – The Plan
XVI	–	Locating The Threat	123
XVII	–	Taking The First Step…In The Opposite Direction	129
XVIII	–	Brothers and Sisters	133

Outro: Practice What You Preach — 139

6 Love Is Here: A Teenager's Call to (Outstretched) Arms

intro: **Get Real**   July 16, 2009

It's around 9 pm. I'm still a little soggy from my evening swim. I'm on vacation, and I'm writing to you. It's a beautiful summer night here in Florida. I'm currently staying in my grandparents' condo overlooking the Atlantic Ocean. Today, I saw five six-foot long sharks swimming ten feet from shore. They swam right into two innocent people. The people freaked out, but the sharks just kept swimming. Nobody got hurt.

That story has absolutely nothing to do with what I want to talk to you about. I know what you're thinking, but hey, you'd be just as excited as me if you had witnessed a near life-altering shark attack. Anyways, today I was working on an outline for this book. I just finished it this evening. As of right now, I have not begun the actual writing process, and honestly, I'm not sure exactly what I'm gonna say. Like I said, I only have an outline. I just feel like God is leading me to write this. So what is "this" all about? Well, this past year God has been doing some serious remodeling of my heart. He's not done yet. I'm thankful that He is still working on me.

I said He has been working on me for a year. So why did it just start a year ago? I mean, I've been a believer since I was 6. How come God just decided to do something ten years later? The fact is: I didn't let Him. I didn't want God to change my heart. I was comfortable where I was. I didn't care who I was hanging out with. I didn't care what words were coming out of my mouth. I didn't care about what terrible things were filling my head. I just simply did not care. Sounds like typical adolescence, doesn't it? Don't misunderstand me. I tried to be a good Christian. I went to church and youth group, and I sometimes even enjoyed it. I tried to not be as bad as other kids my age, and I succeeded. It wasn't hard to live above society's low expectations. You know, I even paid attention in church. I understood the messages. I agreed with them. I even tried to apply them to my life. But it never worked out for me. Why? Because my heart was never open. My heart was closed to anyone who wanted to do anything with it. Therefore, nothing could be done.

I built up my idols with pride. One was my music collection. I had downloaded much of the collection off the internet. Then, on a particular day last summer, I stopped, and I looked at my sin. It disgusted me, so I vowed to tear down the idols I had built. I went on the computer and immediately deleted all the music I had acquired illegally. Interestingly enough, after deleting the music, I was left with a majority of Christian music. On that day, I dedicated myself to change. I invited God into my heart to change me and mold me into the man He yearned for me to be. My heart was open.

Now I want to ask you, have you been in that place and made that decision? If you haven't, I want you to tear down your idols. Tear down those things that have a hold on your heart, and let God take over. Invite Him to change your heart. Tell Him you will do whatever He tells you to do. Listen to His voice right now. Hear His plea for your heart. Answer the call. Do exactly what He tells you. Open your heart in this moment. Please, don't hold back. If your heart is not in the right place, if you don't tear down your pride, your idols, right now, this book isn't going to do a thing for you. In order for God to work through these words, your heart must be open and eager for change. Dwell on Him in this moment. When you're ready, and only then, turn the page and start your journey. I'm doing this with you. I still need to write the rest of this book. I'm gonna do my very best to write exactly what I feel God is leading me to say. *Lord, we devote ourselves to You right now.*

10 Love Is Here: A Teenager's Call to (Outstretched) Arms

Part One: **THE PEOPLE**

12 Love Is Here: A Teenager's Call to (Outstretched) Arms

1. Our Role As Teenagers

How did you get this book? Take a moment and let that sink in. Maybe a pastor, friend, family member, or mere acquaintance gave or recommended it to you. Maybe you just saw it and decided to pick it up. Maybe it fell out of the sky into your hands. Or maybe someone shoved it in your face and said, *You really need this*. Whatever the case may be, it is undoubtedly in your hands, and you are reading these words. So why *are* you reading these words? Maybe it's because you were told you to at least read the first chapter. In that case, you're stuck reading this for a few more minutes. I also believe there are some of you who really desire understanding. You're confused. You don't understand why God made you a teenager. But He has, and there's no way out of it. Maybe you're saying, *I don't understand myself*. I say that all the time. The apostle Paul said the same thing (Romans 7:15). You, Paul, and I don't get why when we aim to do something good, we end up doing what we hate. We think we know what we're doing, but then it all goes wrong. We're missing something.

Society's Bad Name Given To Us

I'm writing specifically to guys and girls my own age: teenagers. However, I believe that anyone can apply this message. We often are led to understand that teenagers are what they are. Society labels us as "good-for-nothing." We don't even need anyone to say it. Society reeks of it. Teens have their own music, TV shows, and video games. Not only does society eagerly give teens the means for laziness, but society also expects teens to invest time and money into these things. As soon as we become teenagers, we immediately inherit a bad reputation consisting of idleness, laziness, and a nature prone to alcohol and drug abuse, sexual sin, violence, and rebellion. Teenagers are what they are. But this can't be who we are, *right*?

Overcoming Society Through Christ

Sadly, society's view of the average teenager is not mere cynicism. Every teenager is exposed to at least one of the various immoralities mentioned above. Some of us struggle daily with these issues, and relying on our own strength, we will only amount to society's expectation of a good-for-nothing teenager. But we have hope. Jesus says, "…take heart, because I have overcome the world" (John 16:33). The power to overcome society and rise above our dirt reputation is available to us in Christ. He commands us to be in the world, not of the world. He doesn't just say it either. He gives us the strength to accomplish it in Him. If we put our faith in Him and obey His commands, then we can become His children. This is important: If we are not children of God, we are good for nothing.

Freedom In Christ

So what if we *do* want to be His children, and follow His commands? What comes next? One word: freedom. As teenagers, we are well acquainted with this idea. We want to be able to do what we want when we want. We want to be able to make our own choices. We want to be able to choose the direction of our lives. I'm guessing most of us have one, if not all, of those desires. I think you'd be surprised to find that this is really a quite limited view of freedom. When you become a child of God, you receive freedom in Christ. Let me explain.

First, Christ gives you the strength to stop sinning. "Humanly speaking, it is impossible", Christ declares, "But with God everything is possible" (Matthew 19:26). You come before God, confess your sins to Him, and say, *Jesus, forgive me. I never want to do this again. Give me the strength to never return to this sin.* Then you do the hardest part: repent. Repenting means putting everything you have into quitting a particular sin. There will be suffering. Make no mistake about it. But Christ has suffered so that you could have victory over sin. So if you say, *God, I just don't have the strength to stay out of this sin. It's just too much. I know you'll forgive me, so I want to say sorry ahead of time*, you're just telling Jesus, *I know you suffered, but you didn't suffer enough to save me*. We are avoiding our own minimal suffering while telling Jesus He suffered and died in vain. Whether our sins are big or little, we have victory over them. Vomit the poison and don't go back to suck it up. Compromise is the main weapon of the enemy. Don't say, *This thing I'm doing isn't really that bad. I mean, I know Jesus never did it, but I'm not Jesus so I can't be expected to stop this thing.* Poison is poison. Sin is fatal in large or small concentrations. Killing somebody is no worse than using foul language or telling an inappropriate joke. I'm not saying this to convict you. I only mean to point out that we all need saving, and we need to repent of all sin and turn to God (Matthew 3:2).

So, what else comes with being a child of God? Our eyes are fully opened.

We are born spiritually blind. We can't see the impact of our sin in our own lives and in the lives of others. But Christ is all about making the blind see. He says that He has come "to give sight to the blind" (John 9:39). As He gives us sight, we begin to see God in everything. If you have not been in that place, then you won't understand. Those who have will testify that God's ways are awesome. With opened eyes, we fall more in love with our Father as we see Him work. The truth becomes clear. Jesus explains, "Those who walk in the darkness cannot see where they are going. ...I have come as a light to shine in this dark world, so that all who put their trust in me will no longer remain in the dark" (John 12: 35, 46). No longer do we have to wonder why we never get it right. As Christ opens our eyes, we begin to distinguish between the light and the dark. *Thank you, Jesus!*

Not only do children of God have the ability to stop sinning and distinguish between the light and the dark, but they also receive total independence from the world and total dependence on their loving Father. Now, I have to admit that sometimes I can be overconfident in myself. You see, I highly value independence, meaning I don't like to be told what to do. I am a "traditionalist boss". I like making my own decisions. Guess what? So does God. Yeah, that's right. God wants you to make your own decisions. In fact, God delights in you every moment you decide to live for Him. How we live is entirely up to us. God gives His children freedom to make their own decisions.

When we are in Christ, the world cannot touch us. So there is nothing to fear as children of God. We receive independence from society: No longer can society determine our name. When we are adopted into Christ's family, He gives us new names. Let me assure you, the Father's name for you is not "you good-for-nothing teenager." As we obey the Father's voice in our lives, we look forward to the day when He calls us "my good and faithful servant" (Matthew 25:21). When we go from teenager to child of God, we cease to live by our old name, "good-for-nothing teenager", and begin to live by our new name, "good and faithful servant".

Accepting God's Call On Our Lives, His Name For Us, And Our New Role

As teenagers, we have a new name, a new role, and a calling not reserved for a future time when society considers us mature, but for right now. God offers this to teens. God doesn't say, *I'm gonna start taking your life seriously when you become an adult.* God wants to be walking side by side with you right now. He wants to be guiding you through the ups and downs, and if you let Him in, you won't have to figure anything out in your own strength. For instance, God doesn't say, *You know, Zach, that's great you want to walk with me, but I'm gonna let you figure out this whole name business. I'm just gonna step away over here and let you figure out how to be my good and faithful servant.* No, that's not what God says at all. God says, *Zach, I'm going to walk close beside you. I'm going to teach you how to honor me. When you stumble, I will pick you up. When you've been walking so long you can't keep going, I will carry you. And I will never leave you. Because I love you, Zach.* He has called you to walk with Him for the rest of your life and into eternity. Are you gonna accept the call? Or maybe you're gonna hit the reject button because you're tired of God pestering you. God's given you the freedom to choose Him or reject Him; to accept your new name or reject it; to accept your calling to walk with Him or reject it.

II. Our Battlefield: Today's Culture

We've accepted God's call on our lives. We have devoted ourselves to Him alone. We have been drafted into the Army of Christ's Kingdom. He has already placed us deep within enemy territory. We are outnumbered in the battlefield. Culture is against us. Society uses culture to make teens what they are. We are the targets. We've given our lives to Christ. We've submitted to Him. We are being used for His purposes, but our culture is determined to see our downfall. *We* are determined to press on towards the prize (Phil 3:14). The battle commences.

Under Attack By Evil Influences

The enemy is evil. He influences our culture with evil. Culture influences teens with evil. Teens reflect this evil. So what are these evil influences? Just look at the problems society has with teens. Violence is common inside and outside high schools. Foul language is even more common. To make matters worse, sexual sin, such as lust, is most common among teenagers. Why? Sadly, the answer is quite obvious: the culture encourages it. The media is the most notorious offender. Music, movies, TV shows, and video games often incorporate one, if not all three, of these evil influences in order to satisfy teens. This is a serious problem. Media is a large part of the teenage life. What is put into the media is put into the minds of teenagers. Unfortunately, this means that most teenagers are united in sin. Their minds are all filled with the same evil. It's what they've got in common, it's what they talk about, and it's what they put their hearts into. I would rather be utterly alone than united to someone by a bond of sin. It's devastating. The sad truth is that the media doesn't have much of anything pure to offer. Teenagers bathe in the media. If society can see that most teenagers only produce evil, then why is it that we continue to pour evil into their lives? There's a connection here. Teenagers need to be surrounded by influences that honor God. Let's stop fooling ourselves by saying, *Oh, media doesn't affect my heart. Maybe you're that way, but I can handle it.* Let me tell you right now, you can't handle the evil of secular media. I fooled myself for a long time. Give up secular media. Don't let it have any place in your life. I know it's hard. Media is one of the only sources of unity among teens. So it does seem stupid at first to disconnect yourself completely from secular media, and you probably don't like that I'm saying this. I want to dare you to be the one to stand up and speak the truth; the truth that entertaining yourself with any form of sin–I'm talking any foul language, sexual immorality, inappropriate jokes, or violence, whether it be in movies, TV shows, music, video games, books, or just friends–gives God a sick stomach and requires repentance. Are you getting this? I've only mentioned media, and that's only one aspect of culture. Popularity, fitting in, being cool, or whatever you like to call it also encourages sin through drugs, alcohol, clothing, and in living habits. This is the society we live in. This is the culture teenagers must live in. This is the world children of God must be in and not of. This is the battlefield soldiers of Christ's Army must fight upon.

When Flight Is Not An Option

Why must we fight here? Why must this be our battlefield? Evil abounds in our culture. The world of teenagers is overrun by enemy forces. Someone has to fight here. Unfortunately, not all parents are soldiers in Christ's Army. Some are but aren't effective. Still others are mighty warriors who faithfully fight for the advancement of the Kingdom. Those are the few. More are needed. Before you get too excited, I know what you're thinking. To answer your thoughts, there are not enough youth pastors to get the job done. And besides, we need soldiers on the front lines who can directly impact other teens. So who can successfully complete that mission? The answer is you.

When your body senses danger, it releases hormones that trigger a flight or fight response. At that point, you have a decision to make. You must either use that energy to run from the danger, or use it to fight the source of danger. You run away, and either you leave the danger behind you, or the danger follows you, overtakes you, and has its way with you. That's the first option. The second is to stand and fight the danger. The body, in the flight or fight case, is particularly interesting. Under normal conditions you can't physically reach the maximum output of strength. When faced with imminent danger, all of that changes. Hormones can cause muscle fibers to contract like never before if triggered by a perceived threat. This strength cannot be achieved by simple will-power. You have no control over it. It simply comes when you choose to face danger. Of course, the third option is always available. This option consists of freaking out, standing paralyzed in shock, and being dismembered by the enemy.

Right now, you're the front line. Culture is directly in front of you looking *pretty* threatening. You've sensed the danger. Now you have to make a choice.

Option A: You turn around and retreat until the enemy cannot be seen.

Option B: You look the enemy in the eye, and, waving Christ's banner, you charge against the enemy lines, trusting God to give you His strength. You fight.

Option C: You remain afraid. You decide not to take action, and soon enough the enemy has you in his grip.

If you don't decide right now, then you've already picked option C. I would encourage you to go with option B. Paul says, "I have fought the good fight…and I have remained faithful" (II Timothy 4:7). You *will* be victorious, but you must fight.

Fighting The Outside Influences

We've decided to lay our lives on the line for the cause of Christ. Now what? It's not like we can convert secular media. You probably feel like the cause of Christ can't change this culture. I understand. It seems as though the enemy will always control society. You say, *The darkness is so thick. People are lost. They are blind, and they are falling deeper into sin everyday. None of my friends understand the truth. Even if I showed them the light, they wouldn't be able to see it because they can't see. I'll charge the enemy, but it won't matter. My blows will just glance off. Our attack will be useless. What's the point?* I'm quite familiar with those thoughts. The problem is that we haven't made battle plans. Honestly, unless God has already revealed it to you, you have no clue how to fight or even what the fight is about. I'd like to help you understand these issues.

First, why are we fighting? As you probably have witnessed by now, the enemy has twisted this culture with sin. Teenagers encourage each other to sin without even realizing it. This is our fault. This isn't their fault. The enemy has designed a system in which teenagers must rely on culture to enjoy life. The enemy has placed sin as the major factor in the equation. Teenagers do as culture encourages them to do, what they do becomes the "thing to do", and as a result, teenagers encourage each other to sin. But God has called us to be counter-cultural. That's what He's all about, and He wants us to follow after Him in that way. He hasn't called us to wade in shallows; we've been called to dive in the deep end. Some of us aren't great divers. Our entry into the deeps of holiness can be rough, but once we're all in, the water settles and we become used to it. Holiness is the characteristic of being set apart for the purposes of God. Holiness means no compromise with sin. Holiness is being in the world and not of the world. Holiness is one of our main means of attack. I know you're saying, *Hold on Zach, you're giving me a strategy without an objective. What's the objective? What are we trying to accomplish in this fight?*

Look around you. Look through the eyes of Christ. Look into your school, your church, your home. What do you see? So many people are living in spiritual darkness. Teenagers are being held captive by the enemy. They are given weapons and told, *Go fight.* But they don't know who they are fighting. After all, they're blind. They don't know they're marching against Christ's Army. This is how we fight the enemy: we take back his pawns. We invite them to join the advancing Kingdom. I mentioned earlier that one of the main weapons is holiness. We can make a statement to the world by defying our culture. This is the largest counter-cultural movement ever. We turn from our evil ways, those influences in the media and our schools, and we devote ourselves only to what is pure in the Lord's sight. How do we know what's pure? The Bible gives us that answer. Ephesians describes how we should live as Children of the Light. We must trust that what Paul says is from God. Not only do I trust that, but I also believe that these scriptures were written with us in mind. This is God's word to teenagers, to young adults. Read Ephesians 4 and 5. God was thinking of you when He inspired these words in the heart of His servant Paul. If Paul were around today, I think he'd be a youth pastor. He understands our emotions and desires. He understands our trials and temptations. Don't you wish you had someone who could understand your heart? Your wish is about to come true.

I know this guy. He's my best friend. He knows you. He knows you better than you know yourself. Remember the teenage plea of distress: *I don't understand myself.* Jesus understands you when you don't. He's got your best interest in mind. He knows the desires of your heart and yearns to reward those who follow after Him (Psalm 37:4). He has a plan for your life. It's a plan designed specifically for you in order to give you a hope and a future, never to harm you (Jeremiah 29:11). You can trust in this: His plan never fails. As you ask Him to be your best friend, ask Him also for strength to shine a holy light in the darkness, for perseverance as you surround yourself with only what is pure in His eyes. *Lord, I ask You for these things.*

Victory…Kind Of

In most instances, our attack never goes quite the way we planned. As we charge towards the enemy, we encounter a few obstacles: hyper-holiness, loneliness, and dependency. I bet you're scratching your head right now, *What's hyper-holiness? You probably just made it up to make a point.* You should be proud of yourself, smarty-pants. I did, indeed, invent the term, hyper-holiness, to get a point across to you. So now let me tell you what it means.

You may have thought, *God wants me to be holy. He wants me to be set apart for Him completely. So I guess I need to set myself apart from society entirely.* Well, that would be true, but I would become immediately worried for you. We must understand what God envisions when He calls us to be holy, to be set apart for Him, to be in the world not of the world. I'd like you to pay close attention to that phrase "…in the world not of the world." If we go lock ourselves up somewhere, it's true we're less likely to be of the world, but as soon as we do that, we are not in the world anymore. Christ's mission wasn't to make life as easy as possible for us. He commands us to be in the world so that we have to choose Him over the world. In order to be holy you need to be living life with other people. God doesn't desire for you to go form some Holy Christian Community where the goal is to avoid contact with non-believers. We are here to make disciples of non-believers. Therefore, we have to have contact with those that are blind. We have to talk with those that are blind. We have to live with those that are blind. Holiness is about saying no to sin, not saying no to sinners.

The second obstacle is that of loneliness. What I mean by loneliness is the "do-it-on-my-own" renegade attitude. You aren't Rambo. You aren't John Wayne. You can't go into battle on your own if you want victory. Christ has supplied us with an army of believers with the same objective in mind: to make teenage disciples of Christ. It's necessary to join with your fellow soldiers as you charge the enemy. Ecclesiastes 4:12 tells that companions serve as strength against the enemy. 4:10 says that a man needs a brother alongside him to pick him up when he stumbles. This is especially important in battle. You go in alone, you get killed. You need someone to cover your advance. I can tell you're thinking, *I got it. I got it. But I don't have anybody*. If that's the case, ask God to point someone out to you.

The third obstacle, dependency, is a faulty solution to loneliness. Dependency takes the need for fellowship and distorts it into a focus on self rather than on God. It happens when you begin to value the companionship of believers over your companionship with Jesus Christ. This is a dangerous place to be. You are filled with confidence as you approach the enemy. But when you confront the evil one, you find yourself without the supernatural strength you once felt. You are left with your own strength and your companion's strength, and you wonder where God is. Don't let that be you. Dependency upon people is a heart defect. You are meant to be dependent upon God. Jesus says, "…anyone who doesn't receive the kingdom of God like a child will never enter it" (Luke 18:17). He wants you to depend upon Him as a child depends upon his parents. Never forget that you are dependent on Him alone as you fight this battle.

III. Sabotage Of The Heart

This next topic is hard for me to write. I honestly don't know much about it. I've only had so much experience in this area, so I don't want to sound as if I'm an expert. The topic is: The Open Heart. The easiest way to visualize our situation is by imagining open-heart surgery. Obviously, the whole point to open-heart surgery is fixing a serious, often life-threatening, problem inside the heart. We all have a life-threatening problem in our heart. It's called sin. You can choose to either have it fixed or not. If you want to have it fixed, open-heart surgery is required. Now, some people want to fix the problem, but they don't want to open their heart and have somebody actually touch it. These people try to find other methods of fixing the sin problem. These "other methods" often result only in lost awareness of the problem, or in other words, numbness. Others don't even care enough to fix the problem. They are comfortable living in sin and do not want to consider change. Still some teenagers, like you and me, desire open-heart surgery.

There are many surgeons out there. They would all like to open your heart. It's up to you to choose who performs your surgery. God wants to be your "surgeon". He wants you to open your heart to Him alone. He wants you to trust Him to fix the sin problem. The eternal destiny of your life is determined by this "surgery". You must decide to whom you open your heart. Whomever you choose has the power to fix the sin problem or make it worse.

If we are to give our lives to Jesus, we must choose to open our hearts to Him alone, ask Him to do whatever is necessary to fix the problem, and accept that we are dead to sin; that sin no longer has a place in our hearts; that Jesus Christ has left His mark permanently on our hearts.

Our Vulnerable Position

As soon as we decide to open our hearts to Jesus, we are in an extremely vulnerable position. Think about it. When our hearts were closed, no evil influence could come in and make it any worse. The tricky thing was that we knew sin was eating away at our hearts, and the longer we remained closed, the more certain our fate of eternal suffering became. So we decided it was necessary to open our hearts to Christ. He knocked on our hearts' door, and we invited Him to dwell in us forever, permanently taking away our heart defect known as sin (Revelation 3:20).

We now realize that our hearts are exposed to evil influences like never before. The enemy sees the open door and makes plans to steal, kill, and destroy (John 10:10). This is where the saying, "guard your heart" comes from. I know it's cliché, but it's true. This is unique to children of

God. Our hearts are open, thus we must guard against invaders (Proverbs 4:23). Those who are not children of God do not need to guard their hearts because their hearts are already closed. They are dying because sin still reigns in their hearts. We are just beginning to live because Christ is doing a work in our hearts. This work will end in perfection, not on earth, but when we meet our Savior in all His glory (Phil 1:6). This is our hope. To see this accomplished, we must guard our hearts against enemy attacks. And the enemy *will* attack.

Enemy Strategies

Currently, Christ is reigning in our hearts. We have died to sin, and we live entirely for Christ who saved us. We are children of God, committed to following Him wherever He leads and obeying all His commands. In the meantime, the enemy waits to strike. His plan is simple: send invaders into our hearts and send Jesus out. Who are the invaders? They are those persons, places, things, or ideas that attempt to take priority over Christ. Another name for an invader is an idol. Idols can be anything from relationships to sports, media to food, popularity to fame, or comfort to wealth. The enemy can send nearly anything to your heart's door with the intention of taking the place of Christ. They look appealing, and sometimes we think we need them. Compromise is easy when we have an attractive visitor wanting a place in our heart. It's easy to say, *But if I had this, I could live for Christ even better*, or, *This little thing has nothing to do with Christ in my heart. It won't even make a difference*. It always makes a difference. All the enemy needs is for you to allow an idol one step into your heart. We must not let any idol enter. You must say, *This is Christ's home. You don't belong here. In His name, don't come here again*. It's okay to tell idols off.

Ask Christ for protection. He will stand guard at the door, giving you the strength to say no (Phil 4:7). In the end, it's up to you who you let into your heart. Be careful, be firm. Guard your heart.

Desire Is Not Evil

Desire is normal. If you have a heart, you have desires. Some desires are common to all humans. These are natural desires such as the desire for food or the desire for sleep. Then there are the desires that are unique to our personalities. These are personal desires such as the desire to play sports or the desire to listen to music. There is one more category of desires. These are the desires of your heart, or spiritual desires. These are the desires that Jesus promises to give His followers. God doesn't care so much about our desire for food as He does our desire to be content with what we are given. God doesn't care so much about our desire for sleep as He does our desire for peace and true rest. God doesn't care so much about our desire for romantic relationships as He does our desire for true companionship and fellowship. Are you getting the picture? God's into the heart. And no, there's no way of organizing your heart's desires to get what you want of your natural or personal ones. Your heart's desires make up the foundation upon which all your personal desires are built.

Your heart's desires even coincide with your natural desires. Let's say for instance you desire sleep. What does your heart desire? Rest and peace in Christ? Or a break from your hard life? Or let's say you desire food. Does your heart desire energy to live for Christ? Or satisfaction and the good feeling of being full? I'm not a scientist, so I'm not familiar with the science of desires. All I'm saying is that God has created us in a way such that our hearts can reveal what we truly desire. Our heart's desires can be pure or evil. Christ will honor our pure desires, but our evil desires are sin.

It's common to have evil desires. These desires result from invaders, idols. But there is hope. As long as we are in Christ, we are no longer slaves to these evil desires, the desires of our flesh.

Christ Is The Solution

So Zach, you're saying that if we are children of God, we don't ever have to worry about evil desires, right? Unfortunately, no. All through the Christian walk, we will find ourselves battling evil desires. The problem isn't that we're not godly enough. Jesus Christ was tempted with the same evil desires that we face. He overcame all of them. He did not give in once. He guarded His heart against evil desires, and they could not touch Him. Christ gives us the strength to resist temptation just as He did (Hebrews 4:15, 2:18).

First, eliminate the source of the desire if possible. Now, if the source is a person, please don't eliminate that person. A good alternative would be to avoid that person, and find someone who encourages pure desires (II Timothy 2:22).

Second, focus your mind on what is good, praiseworthy, and true (Phil 4:8). Dwell on your pure Savior. If you fill your mind with what is pure, it will be much harder for evil desires to form any significant presence in your life.

Last, but most important, continually ask Jesus for strength to resist temptation Ask Him to give you pure desires and defeat the evil ones.

32 Love Is Here: A Teenager's Call to (Outstretched) Arms

Part Two: **THE PASSION**

34 Love Is Here: A Teenager's Call to (Outstretched) Arms

IV. The Design Of The Heart

Look around you. Look at your friends. Look at the kids in the hallways at school. Look at the Christians in your youth group. Look in the mirror. What do you see? You probably see some "good-for-nothing" teenagers. The most prominent image isn't the most pleasant. It's really disgusting when you think about how we glorify sin many times without knowing it. I once heard someone say that we are "made to love". Can we really believe that teenagers are made to love? If you don't believe it, I don't blame you. It's hard to believe something when you can find little or no proof. I want you to understand that we teenagers, believers and non-believers, are truly made to love.

Each and every heart is unique. All hearts, however, are designed to operate the same way. The function of our hearts is to love, to love our

Savior, to love our Creator, and to love our neighbor. Some hearts function properly. Others don't. But when our hearts are functioning properly, the result is love. No matter who you are, you are capable of loving, even if you're a "good-for-nothing" teenager.

Meant To Work Selflessly

Those who are children of God desire to love others. *What does that look like?* I'm glad you asked. The most important thing you need to know about love is that it is always selfless. For those of you who don't know, selflessness is the opposite of selfishness. This means that when you choose to love, you are not after personal gain in any way. In fact, love is often an inconvenience to yourself with the purpose of blessing someone else. Sometimes we are drawn to love certain people over others. I think that's true for all of us. We have to make a practice of loving the unlovable. Jesus loved the least of these. He said that when we love those that are hard for us to love, we are really loving Him (Matthew 25:40).

Why am I making such a big deal about love? Because love is what we are called to do. This book is about teenagers accepting the call to love and living it out where God has placed them. *Why not something more specific? Love is so vague, Zach. I want to do something for Christ that's gonna amount to something.* I know you do. So do I. But we have to understand that we're not adults yet. We don't have complete independence. We're not on our own. We're still under the authority of our parents. Therefore, we can't quit school and become missionaries. Don't get me wrong. This isn't an excuse to not minister to people. I'm trying to show you that we have limited independence for a reason. Christ has places to use us while we are teenagers. Love is the foundation of all ministry. This is the time to develop a habit of loving people, particularly the unlovable. Your fellow teenagers, those who are exposed to this twisted culture same as you, those who are blind; they need you to love them. But not so that you can accomplish anything in their lives. God forbid that you'd be able to change their hearts. No, not you but Christ in you. May the blind see Christ in you as He gives you a bright light. Shine, it's your duty (Matthew 5:16).

Desire To Constantly Keep Love In Motion

All right Zach, I understand that love is selfless and that it's my duty to shine the light that Christ has instilled in my heart. But what if I don't feel like it? What if it doesn't come easy? I'm not sure that loving people will ever come easy to any of us. Honestly, it's hard work. Love is hard. Many times, we don't like doing hard things. But I'm gonna suggest to you that love is an acquired desire. You know, like an acquired taste. Have you ever had green tea? It has an interesting taste. Now, I'm not talking flavored green tea. I'm talking straight up natural green tea. The best way I can describe its taste is with the word "earthy". Basically, it's not a taste that everybody enjoys. But the thing about green tea is that it's a very healthy drink. Personally, when I drink green tea, I don't necessarily enjoy the flavor, but it makes me feel good. I develop a desire for green tea because it gives me a good feeling when I've finished. The same is true for exercise. While working out, you must push yourself. You must work hard. But, in the end, you feel good about it. Sometimes it might hurt, but proper exercise rewards you with good health as well as confidence. The same is true for love. It takes hard work to be selfless, but you feel good about it in the end.

Let me ask you something, is it easy to develop and maintain an exercise habit? Do you always feel like working out everyday? Of course not. Loving is a habit that's hard to start and even harder to maintain.

There will be days when you don't feel like loving. As children of God, we must take up our cross daily and follow wherever Christ leads (Luke 9:23). The desire to love others is a precious thing that only Christ can instill. Make a point to serve others joyfully, and you will know this desire. It is a consuming fire that Christ alone can spark in our hearts. Children of God thrive on this desire. Make love a habit, don't give up, and you will experience the desire to continually keep love in motion.

Christ Maintains Function

Remember, a functioning heart results in the output of love. Christ is the only one who can keep your heart functioning. When we connect the dots, we find that only those with Christ in their heart can truly love others. The desire to love is a consuming fire that Christ sparks. Our job is to fan the flame. If we forget the fire, it will die out. We must avoid this. God's word is like the oxygen in fire. It is the fuel. If you want the fire to stay strong, you must stay in the Word. Quiet time with God keeps our heart functioning. If I were you, I'd be saying, *I thought the fire thing was Jesus' job. It's hard enough for me to love the unlovable. Now you're telling me I have to be in the Word daily with a quiet time on top of it.* Yeah, that's what I'm saying. I told you love is hard work. Take a moment and understand that it's really not as bad as it appears. The closer you grow to God, the more you enjoy spending time with Him in His Word and outside it. Don't believe me? When you first met your best friend, did you desire to spend all your time with him or her? You had to get to know that person. It's a process, and it takes time. After awhile, you either find that you really like the person or maybe not so much. I'm asking you to give God a try. There's nothing not to like about Him. There's everything to like about Him.

God wasn't always my best friend. He was a friend ever since I became a Christian, but I never let Him be my best friend. Choose to spend more time with Him. Quiet time is simply hanging out with God. Just talk to Him. No distractions. He likes your attention. Then simply be quiet and listen. God values your time. I dare you to give it to Him generously.

Joy In The Properly Functioning Heart

I bet you'd like to know what good feeling you get from loving others. When I choose to love others, I find myself feeling an abundance of joy. It's a feeling of contentment mixed with a love for life. Joy is a gift only God can give. It's always a surprise. It catches you off guard. You can't anticipate it. It's impossible to expect ahead of time. It's a beautiful feeling. It doesn't last forever. It's a high that you get by loving selflessly. I can't get over the fact that joy is so unexpected. It comes when you are lost in love. Lost. When you're devoted to living apart from yourself. Love is selflessness; selflessness results in joy. Teenagers are made to love. Teenagers are made to receive joy from nothing more than functioning properly. God designed you this way. Take the difficult steps. Follow His design: your heart.

40 Love Is Here: A Teenager's Call to (Outstretched) Arms

V. The Broken Heart

The Beginnings

In the last chapter, we discussed what a properly functioning heart looks like. But, why do we have to work so that our heart loves? I mean if we were made to love, why isn't that how our heart functions at first? Well, God originally had it that way. Both Adam and Eve were created with hearts that loved naturally. The problem came when they gave in to temptation. Sin entered their hearts. They fell off the mountaintop where they once lived with God. As a result of the fall, we now have to start in the valley and journey our way to the mountaintop through faith.

Born Broken

Adam and Eve were the only humans ever brought into this world with properly functioning hearts. They did not have the sin problem eating away at their hearts until they let sin enter by disobeying God. The penalty? We are born broken. It's not something we can avoid. We arrive in this world with the sin problem already in our hearts, ready to deliver us into eternal death. This is where we all start. It marks the beginning of a period of blind wandering. Until we become children of God, we are stuck with a heart that doesn't work. We can't love until we get a working heart. We become desperate. Some of us can remember being in this place. Others who are reading this are in that place right now. Take a moment. Be sure you know if you have a working heart or not.

Operating The Failing Machine

When you realize something is broken, what do you do? Hopefully, you try to fix it. At a certain point in time, we realize our hearts aren't working. *Something must be wrong. How come I can never love people the right way?* I believe that's a common and important question we ask ourselves. It shows that we desire a working heart. So what *is* wrong? We're trying to operate a machine with its most important part missing. There's only one solution to this problem. We need to find that missing piece and plug it in.

I've already told you the story. We've been born with a heart disease called sin. We need the anti-body. We desire a functioning heart. The antibody for sin is the only way to fix it. We need forgiveness. We need a fresh start. We're desperate for the missing piece. *Lord, give us the cure.* He already has. It's Jesus Christ.

Installing The Missing Piece

Jesus Christ is the missing piece. We are born with a heart unable to truly love. Our heart is designed to love, but without the missing piece, we are unable to love despite our strongest efforts. When we ask Christ to live in our hearts, He enters and begins the process of molding us into perfection. Even children of God were once unable to love. If you desire eternal life, you must let Christ fix your heart.

Sin will always exist in this world, but it has no place in your heart. You cannot take care of your heart's sin problem by your own efforts. We all need to ask Jesus to fix our sin problem. When we do, we become children of God, our eyes open, and we can see God for who He is as we develop a personal relationship with Him who saved us. This is where we should strive to arrive at as teenagers. If you're there already, praise God! If you're not, make the decision to give your heart to Christ today, and get ready to take the next step, children of God (Romans 5:19).

44 Love Is Here: A Teenager's Call to (Outstretched) Arms

VI. The Teenage Heart

Before we take a step further, I want us to step out of the scene for a moment. Look at yourself. Look at those around you. Look passed appearances. Look at the heart. As teenagers, we sometimes appear to not have a care in the world. Let's remove that façade. There must be a reason why we do what we do. There must be a driving force behind all of our actions. You heard me. All of them. What is the typical teenage response to the question, *why'd you do that?* Isn't it, *Just cause?* Maybe we say it because we don't like to explain ourselves. Or maybe we say it because we don't have an explanation. We don't know why we do what we do. It would be worth it to learn what drives you. Trust me.

What We Care About

We've paused time. We're looking at ourselves frozen in life. So let me ask you, what do you care about? Do you care about money, social status, power, adventure, fun, romance, relationships, health, nature, popularity, or maybe the well-being of other people? Whatever it is we care about, it always influences our actions. If you're trying to "fit in", you care about acceptance, popularity, relationships, or any number of things. The idea is that something is driving you to "fit in". What I want you to understand is that as teenagers, if we want to fit in, we're going to put our whole selves into accomplishing that goal. Whether our motives are good or evil, we are determined to see it happen. This doesn't just apply to fitting in. It applies to being wealthy, having a relationship, and finding adventure. It applies to everything.

As teenagers, we push ourselves to get what we want. You're saying, *Zach, I don't push myself towards anything. I just do whatever I feel like.* If you sit on the couch and play video games or watch TV, you are devoting yourself to a life of fun and ease. You can't escape the truth that you are always pushing yourself towards an ideal that you've crafted out of the cares of your heart. This applies to everyone. It's how God made us. Whether our priorities are straight or not, we care, and we can't help it.

We Have A Voice

We care. I get it. But we're teenagers, so we can't care a whole lot. On the contrary, I think teenagers *can* care a whole lot. But I understand why you'd say that. Society usually doesn't care if we care. When there are issues, society appeals to adults because adults care. Society doesn't want to listen to the voice of a teenager. We all have opinions. We all have a voice. But society doesn't want you to care. It certainly doesn't want you to care about things that are important. Teenagers are trouble. Who would value their cares? That's why we've decided to break away from our reputation, why we've rejected society's name for us, why we've accepted our name from God, why we've embraced God's call to be His "good and faithful servants". Now we can raise our voice with integrity. Society will hear our cries, and the world will have no choice but to listen to our shouts of praise to our Savior, Jesus Christ.

Understanding Our Potential

Ever since we became teenagers, society has told us: 1) That we don't care, so we live carelessly; 2) That even if we did care, we have no voice; and 3) That even if we did have a voice, no one would listen to a "good-for-nothing" teenager. I bet you've got a few things you want to tell society right now. Before you get too excited, you should understand your potential and learn to be responsible with your voice.

Why do you think society, under the influence of the enemy, wants to keep teenagers silent? Think about it for a minute. I began this book telling you to get real. The enemy doesn't want teenagers to get real. He wants you to remain immature. Once you get real about life, once you open your heart to the healing power of Christ, you become a threat to the enemy. You strengthen the Army of Christ. You begin to fight for the Kingdom. The Kingdom of Christ is the nightmare of the enemy. It signifies the end to his reign and the beginning of Christ's reign in the world. Let Christ reign in your heart and the enemy is weakened. As a teenager, you have to make the decision to get real or not. That's why society wants to keep teenagers believing they don't have a care in the world. The longer society can keep you from maturing, the less of a threat you are to the enemy. That's why society wants to keep you silenced. The second you realize you have a voice and that it will be heard, you throw off your childish ways and become a man or woman of God (I Corinthians 13:11).

Society has gagged you, and you don't even know it. Ask Jesus to take the gag off, and you will find your voice. If the enemy keeps you silent through your teenage years, he starts to gain ground. It gets harder to find your voice as you get older. Now's the time to strike the enemy a blow he will never forget. There's a whole company of teenagers waiting to release their voice and join the cause of Christ. Be the one to start the revolution against society. You have the potential to ignite a chorus of teenage voices shouting praise to the One who has rescued them from darkness. All you have to do is raise your voice, acknowledge that you care, acknowledge Christ as your driving force, and He will give you the strength to do His will.

Devoting Our Whole Selves

Teenagers are strong soldiers. We fight tooth and nail. However, we can easily make a wrong turn. Teenagers often lash out at society with a voice of rebellion. Sometimes we get so caught up in what society has done to us, we forget to use our voices to praise God, and instead we fight evil with evil. Violence, drugs and alcohol, and all forms of abuse often result from anger at society. People think they can fight society this way, but it only helps the enemy. He wants teenagers to rebel because it helps him give society reason to imprison teens. I don't mean putting teens behind physical bars, but rebelling against society allows society to justify silencing teenagers, making them think they are worthless kids, and keeping them from getting real.

This is why we're called to a revolution of love. I know I'm being cliché again, but it's true. Love is the only way to defeat society. As teenagers fighting for Christ, our goal is to love others with the hope that more teenagers will join the cause. We'll never know exactly how God's gonna work, but we know He's called us to make disciples through the love of Jesus Christ.

50 Love Is Here: A Teenager's Call to (Outstretched) Arms

Part Three: **THE PROBLEM**

52 Love Is Here: A Teenager's Call to (Outstretched) Arms

VII. Carried Away

We've made the decision to raise our voices of love to our broken society. Those with ears to hear must choose to join Christ's Army or be used by the enemy. Our goal is always before us: to make disciples of our fellow teenagers (Matthew 28:19). It's an exciting mission that God has called us to. Do you see it? Can you see the prize? I can see it: Teenagers turning away from sin, away from the media that seeks to pollute our minds, away from the garbage, away from everything impure the world has to offer, away from the mainstream, away from the norm, away from the names we've been given by society, away from the prison that held us captive, away from the idols we used to worship, away from half-hearted faith, away from all that is fake, away from the pleasure of the flesh, away from evil and unimportant desires, away from complacency, away from seeing things from an earthly perspective, away from the lies of the world.

I see an exodus of teenagers from the slavery of sin. We're dropping our fishing nets. We're leaving all we've ever known. We're abandoning all we ever thought was important. We're leaving it all behind to follow where Christ leads, all because He has called us by name (Matthew 4:19-20, Isaiah 43:1). I see Him dwelling in our hearts, giving us life, and giving us a reason to actually live. This is our vision. This generation of teenagers will start a revolution. We will unite to fight for our freedom.

So here we are. Love is our weapon and we're targeting relationships; relationships with those who are children of God and those who are not. Here we encounter a problem. You see, we're teenagers. We aren't the best at relationships. I think we'd all have to admit that sometimes we feel like we've wasted time on someone, or that someone has wasted our time. Maybe I'm off target, but I feel like teenagers and wisdom in relationships are two ideas that seem to clash. Relationships is the main theme of this book. It's why I'm writing to you. I know I need help, and I think many of us are in the same boat. So let's get some help, shall we?

Getting Close Enough To Love

There's this rumor going around about some requirements to be able to love. For instance, *It's necessary to be someone's close friend to be able to really love that person.* It would be easy for us to believe this, but it isn't true. Close friends are a blessing from God, but they aren't necessary for the love of Christ to work.

We often think that we have to get close enough to love. We think we need to have contact with someone's heart in order to love them. We're fooling ourselves. It's not out job to touch someone's heart. That's Christ's job.

If we get close to someone, we're actually getting into risky business. I understand that it doesn't make sense. Common sense would say that the more contact you have with someone's heart, the better ability you have to love that person, because love is heart to heart. Love *is* heart to heart. The heart both gives and receives love. *So we need to get really close so that our hearts can exchange love, right?* Wrong. But you continue, *No Zach, it only makes sense. If I want to love someone, I need to open my heart to that person so the love can come out. Then that person needs to open their heart to me so that my love can enter their heart. I know I'm right, Zach. I figured it out.* Well, that makes sense. It's logical. But you're missing the main part of the heart.

Remember when we talked about Jesus being the missing piece that allows the heart to function? To love? Jesus is the heart guy. He lives in hearts. He fixes hearts. He treasures hearts. He is the owner of hearts. The heart is His place, not ours. We stay out of it and let Him take over. Don't ever try to take Jesus' place in someone's heart. It's a trap. That person won't receive any love if you do, you'll only screw them up worse. You have to accept the fact that Jesus has a monopoly over the heart business, and you've got no share in it.

It's actually a great relief. Jesus worries about the hearts of other people so we don't have to. Our job is to obey Him as He speaks to our hearts. *Zach, you've made such a big deal over loving people and now you're warning me to stay away, or else. How on earth am I supposed to love now?* God is love. He wants to use you to make Himself real in people's hearts. You don't have to get close to people for God to use you. As you have contact with people under normal conditions, Christ can allow people to see Him through you. As Christ uses you, people won't fall more in love with you, they will fall more in love with Christ. Don't ask me how it happens. I cannot possibly understand the awesome ways of God. But I know that when Christ shines through normal Christians, people are brought out of the darkness and devote themselves to Him, not to you or me, but to Jesus Christ, the One who saved them. So don't *try* to be intimate with people. Just let Christ work through you. This is selflessness. We know that He "must become greater and greater", and we "must become less and less" (John 3:30).

As teenagers, we must value the relationships God gives us, and avoid imposing intimacy upon them. Let Christ work in your friends' hearts. Those hearts aren't yours to mess with, they are the property of God. Let Him use you. Always say yes to the voice of God. Don't try to do anything without the guiding voice of God.

Loving Without Boundaries

Teenagers don't like boundaries. I would know. I am a teenager. We frequently, when faced with difficult situations, come to the conclusion that the world would be a better place if we could all just do whatever we want. The truth is that the world would have to be a better place if we were allowed to do whatever we want. Unfortunately, we live in a fallen world, so we can't do whatever we want. Therefore, we must set up boundaries to determine what we can and cannot do.

Consider, for a moment, love without boundaries. At first, that sounds pretty good. It would be like selflessness galore. Everyone would be putting others first. Sounds delightful. Sadly, we can't count on everyone to stick with this plan. Along the way, someone is bound to take advantage of our selflessness. We find ourselves in a bit of a pickle. Despite our predicament, we have hope in Christ. You see, God knows that we don't live in a utopia. He knows that we are all born with a sinful nature, and that even children of God do evil sometimes. He knows that people will take advantage of selflessness. Lucky for us, God gives us a tool to let us know when we're taking selflessness too far: the Holy Spirit, the voice of God in our hearts.

Our selflessness, our love, is modeled after Christ. He didn't come to earth to satisfy all our desires. Neither should we aim to satisfy others' desires out of love. Christ calls us to put others first, not worship them. Christ alone deserves worship.

I can't tell you exactly when selflessness becomes people-worship. I don't think there's an absolute answer to that. I can only suggest that you read the Bible *a lot*. Get to know your Savior so that you'll know how He would respond in all situations. And when you are confronted with a situation you question, stop and pray about it immediately. God doesn't want you to mess up. He'll help you know what choice is true love.

Valuing Love Over Truth

There comes a time when we must decide whether the love we are receiving or giving is, in fact, biblical love.

This is the debate of Truth v. Love. Truth is biblical love. The world has a way of twisting biblical love. This false love is accepted by society. Therefore, when we do something out of biblical love, let's say correction, the world tells us it's not love, and we are looked upon as unloving. Or let's say we don't do something because we know it's not biblical. Well, then the world tells us we've fallen short of true love. We have to stay true to the truth; the truth of love that's found only in God's Word.

The world loves worldly love. The world hates biblical love (II Corinthians 15-16). Many people don't always appreciate true love. Sometimes it hurts and it's disappointing, but it's the kind of love the world needs, and it's the only love that saves. So hold on to the truth, and stand firm when the world wants to see you fall in worldly love.

Blurring Lines

We're holding on to the love of Christ with everything we have. But it's hard. We feel like our strength is weakening. Our grip is loosening. We're afraid that we're gonna fall out of the love of Christ. Desperate, we think there's only one option: blur the lines. We think that if we give ourselves just a little extra rope, just a little leeway, then we'll have enough strength to press on.

I cannot tell you how easy it is to convince ourselves of this. It doesn't even feel like compromise. We think that we can just give in to worldly love a little bit and we'll be able to regain the needed strength to stand for Christ's love. It may seem silly now, but trust me, when you're worn out from Christ's love, it doesn't look like a bad option. Our hearts are tired (II Corinthians 6:10). It's true. We need some sort of rest. We are in love with Christ. We value His love above all else, but we won't make it if we don't get relief. That's the situation. But there's more to it for us teenagers. When we understand what's really happening, we'll find our hope.

There's a light at the end of the tunnel, and it's closer than you think.

VIII. The Teenage "Needs"

Has anyone ever called you "needy"? I'm guessing that if your answer is yes, then you probably were somewhat offended by that derogatory term. Well, I think you're needy. Don't take it personally. I think we're all needy. Most teenagers would probably deny the fact. Whether you knew so or not, I'm asking you to accept that you *are* needy. *Okay Zach, thanks for making me feel terrible about myself. Now what's your point?* Hold on a minute. Being needy doesn't have to be a bad thing, and remember the common trend of hope that's developing. We're needy, and we seek to satisfy those needs. The way we satisfy our needs is the most important thing. We must turn somewhere. But where?

We're Just In That Awkward Stage

We've had needs ever since we were born. When we were younger, we didn't have to worry about meeting our needs. That was our parents' job. If you were raised in a family like mine, you could rely on your parents to meet your needs.

Some needs go away with age, but others last a lifetime. These lifetime needs include love and affection, security, comfort, entertainment, companionship, and the obvious ones like food, shelter, and clothing. I want us to focus on those first five lifetime needs. I know some of you didn't have these needs met when you were a child. I can't relate to that. The majority can't relate to that. But this is still for all of us. We all need to understand where we're currently at even though we've come from different places. I'm going to progress from where I've come from, so just track with me.

When we were kids, I don't think boredom felt that bad. I mean, I think lots of teenagers struggle with boredom that actually hurts. When we were kids, it was easier to entertain ourselves, and if we couldn't, someone would do it for us. It may just be me, but I feel like parents aren't as good at entertaining teenagers as they are with kids. Or it might be that we just get harder to entertain as we get older. Anyways, the point is we have this need for entertainment and suddenly as teenagers we're having a much more difficult time filling that need.

We'll come back to this later, but for now you just need to understand why we're looking to satisfy these needs.

Okay, let's move on. Companionship. We start to get a little more personal with this one. It's possible that you've struggled with this your whole life. What is "this"? It's loneliness. We want somebody to do life with. While we're kids, acceptance is easier. It gets harder as we get older.

People become more judging, more selective of friends. When we were kids, some of us at least always had our parents as friends. When we become teenagers, many of us don't want our parents as companions. We become more selective, and they aren't what we're looking for. But we still desire companionship. We desire it now more than ever. So we keep looking.

The next need is comfort. We want to feel good. Maybe as kids, we thought our parents didn't care about our comfort at times, but I think they did their best. Guess what happens as we get older? Yep, you guessed it: our need for comfort grows. I believe this one is more natural than the others. As we become teenagers, we start to grow up physically. This can lead to more sensitivity and discomfort. During this time, we're really itching for a deep source of comfort.

Now let's think about security. This is the feeling of safety that gives us peace. Once again, I must take it back to the parents. As kids, we couldn't protect ourselves very well, whether it be against sickness, weather, danger, or our own silly accidents. We relied on our parents and other adults to protect us. As children, our sense of security came from them. You take the parents away without warning and their children panic. They are defenseless because their sense of security comes from the presence of their parents. As we get older, we see the world for what it is: dangerous. I believe we lose our sense of security in our parents as we experience more of life. We ask, *If anything were to happen to me, who would really be there?* So we search for the answer.

This last need is the toughest. It is love and affection. I don't like to be repetitive, but this one really traces back to the parents. When we were young, they were our only source of love and affection. We looked to them, and they satisfied that need. We even returned the blessing. What happened along the way? Now we're teenagers, but where's the love and affection? Maybe there's a certain age where we become to old to cuddle with Mom and Dad, or kiss them goodnight. They were the main source of love and affection, and now many of us have lost them as a source for whatever reason.

I want to make it clear that you can't help it. That's how life works. God didn't design your parents to always fill that need. It's part of His plan that they stop. Unfortunately, that leaves a significant void for us teenagers. The need is strong, so we seek hard to fill it.

The Mistaken Sighting

We all make mistakes, right? Come on, admit it. We get it wrong sometimes. Some mistakes aren't as big as others. Some mistakes don't even affect anything. But I think now's the time when teenagers are most likely to make a big mistake.

The scene is set. We've entered into the awkward stage; the time in our lives when we must search to fill our voids; those left by the flight of our sustenance. As teenagers, we have to find a new source to fill our five major needs. It's easy to choose the wrong source. Here we make a big mistake. We don't do it on purpose. We think we know what we're doing. In fact, we're convinced we've made the right choice. Some of us may say, *I'm a child of God. It's impossible for me to make the wrong choice. God's guiding me, so how can I make a wrong turn?* Many of us believe that. I want to warn you of that mindset right now. I know it feels safe to think that way, but it's actually extremely dangerous.

What's the big deal about making a wrong turn? I call it the "mistaken sighting". We feel like we've found the source that will fill our needs. But we don't fully understand the depth of our needs.

We can resort to many things to fill our needs. Food, drugs, alcohol, recklessness, and violence are all possibilities. I don't know what your personal struggle is. Your "thing" could be anything. I, however, want to focus specifically on relationships. I believe God allows teenagers much time with relationships for a reason. It's how we learn to love. It's the setting in which we show the love of Christ. That's why it's important for those of us who use relationships to fill our needs to start getting it right.

Here's what's happening: God is guiding us along the path of righteousness. Our lifetime needs are weighing heavily upon us, and we're looking around for a source to fill the needs. Then we see a relationship off in the distance. We think, *That must be it. That must be the source that will fill my needs. I know that God isn't exactly in that direction, but He must want me to go that way. I need help. I know that's gonna make me feel better. God wants me to feel better. He wants my needs to be met. I'm His child. That's my only option, or I won't make it much longer.* This whole time our eyes have remained focused on the relationship in the distance. It's attractive. It fools us. We head in the direction of the relationship because we are certain it will feed our needs. We think it's what God wants.

Let me tell you something. The second we took our eyes off our God; the second we took our eyes off our Guide, we lost any chance of filling our needs. If we could have kept both of our eyes on our Savior, He would have led us to the source of satisfaction. But we let our eyes wander because we were desperate, and now we're headed in the direction of destruction. Nothing we find on the way will satisfy our needs. The mistaken sighting has made us take a wrong turn; a turn leading away from the true source.

When The Struggle Never Ends

Now, we're headed towards a person. Our goal is to get close to this person so that one or more of our lifetime needs will be filled. Our attention is on this person, and we are aimed at growing the relationship. We desire satisfaction and as we grow closer, we start to experience this satisfaction on the outside. Isn't it true? We kind of feel satisfied yet at the same time we crave more. What I mean is this: *This person means so much to me, and I wish I could be around them all the time. I know that won't happen, so I'll spend time with them tomorrow, and maybe then I'll be satisfied.* They don't satisfy the need. They become the need.

Those of you who've been in this place know what I'm talking about. It's an addiction. The person is your fix. The person doesn't control the need, the need controls you.

I know what you want to say, *Zach, you tell me these needs will last my entire life. If so, what does true satisfaction look like?* That's an excellent question. Addicts are never truly satisfied because the root problem is never taken care of. Let's say your need is love and affection. You seek a relationship in order to be satisfied. Let me ask you something. Will that person always treat you with love? I know there will come a time when you don't feel loved by that person. Who's faithful enough to love you always? Let's try a different need. How about security? You go to someone because you don't feel safe. That person can make you feel safe, but when it comes down to it, can they really protect you? Tell me, who's powerful enough to raise you from the dead? Or we could even try companionship. We seek out a friend because we want them to be around us. We feel satisfied when we're with them. So now I'll ask you, who can be at your side every second of your life? We value people because they give us a temporary fix. We're addicted to relationships.

Our bodies may be satisfied for now, but our hearts are in anguish. We long for true satisfaction. We want our hearts, not just our minds, to be at peace. We think we're satisfied, but we keep going back for more because we haven't tasted eternal satisfaction. *When will I quit letting my needs dictate my life?*

Prevention Needed

God understands our dilemma. He knows the difference between earthly satisfaction and true satisfaction of the spirit. In fact, Jesus said, "…Anyone who drinks this water will soon become thirsty again. But those who drink the water I give will never be thirsty again. It becomes a fresh, bubbling spring within them, giving them eternal life" (John 4:13-14). Our mistake is that we're satisfied with drinking earthly water even when we soon become thirsty again. If we drank the living water, we would never become thirsty again. This is true satisfaction. Our needs are filled when we go to Christ, but we don't do it.

Even children of God get distracted with the things of this world. How can we keep from making the wrong turn? I already said we need to stay focused on Christ, our Guide. But when we see something attractive in the distance that is not God, we cannot take the second glance. Once you notice a distraction, turn your eyes upon Jesus before it's too late (Proverbs 4:25). We'll talk more about the living water later, but for now always remember to keep your eyes fixed upon Jesus and return to Him the second your mind begins to stray.

IX. The Opposite Sex

Assuming you did not immediately slap this book shut upon reading the chapter title, please hang with me. I know you're probably thinking, *Zach, you can't fool me. You're writing this book to teenagers, you're making love a big deal, and on top of that you're even stressing relationships. I knew what was coming before I even turned the page. So now you're talking about the opposite sex. It's really easy to connect the dots, Zach. I don't need another book about dating.* Yeah, that last word, I'm not gonna use it again in this book. I don't care what your opinions are about it. We're gonna skip right over it. We are going to talk about friendships with the opposite sex, because whether we like it or not, they are different from those with the same sex.

The Strange Attraction

We're all attracted to the opposite sex. Now, I know you might feel the need to disagree with that statement, but I'd ask you to let it go. This is how God has made us, so I'm running with it.

Why does this attraction exist? I think the answer to that question is evident in many cultures and yet often missed. The answer is balance; balance between the masculine and the feminine. We don't always like to admit it, but the masculine and feminine have pros and cons (both, not respectively in case you were wondering). Girls always have feminine hearts and guys always have masculine hearts. This is the work of God.

What are some characteristics unique to the feminine heart? Some could be compassion, tenderness, mercy, or ideas like beauty and admiration. On the other side, strength, protection, competition, ability, and control are all ideas unique to the masculine heart. I know those lists aren't very thorough, but you get the picture. It's not that guys can't be gentle or girls strong, the idea is that some things come naturally to guys and others to girls. God created the two different tendencies to work together towards harmony.

Why are we attracted to the opposite sex? It's because they can make up for your weaknesses. I know some guys are saying, *Weaknesses? I have a masculine heart like God. I don't have weaknesses.* I hate to burst your bubble, but God's heart isn't the same as yours. God has both a masculine and a feminine heart. He possesses both natural tendencies. That's what makes Him perfect. That's why Jesus was perfect as a man. It's impossible for us to have both a masculine and a feminine heart. That's why we're attracted to the opposite sex, and as corny as it sounds, it's because they complete us.

Zach, what does this have to do with what you've been talking about? I see no connection. Well, the connection is especially strong with children of God. We seek to imitate Christ. We want to be more like our Creator (Ephesians 5:1). We find that some of the characteristics of Christ don't come naturally to us. We also find that the opposite sex has what we're looking for. We all know that we act like the people we hang around, right? Well, when we're with the opposite sex, it's easier to experience some of those qualities that are foreign to our heart. There's nothing wrong with this. We need both male influences and female influences in our lives. This helps us achieve the balance of the feminine and masculine hearts.

So that's what we're aiming for. The problem occurs when interacting with the opposite sex. Sometimes our goal of balance gets a little distorted.

Excuses We All Make

We can distort the goal of opposite sex relationships in a few specific ways.

1) Along the way, we start to value the opposite-sex relationships over same-sex relationships. This is not what is supposed to happen. We need same-sex relationships more than opposite-sex ones. Why? Because you can relate to your own gender in ways that you can't with the opposing gender. Being able to relate to a friend about life issues is necessary in growing closer to God. We share with each other in order to learn and grow. You can share anything with the same sex. You can't with the opposite sex. If we start to value the opposite-sex relationships more, then we begin to bottle things up, and then when you finally share, the opposite sex doesn't understand the way the same sex would.

We develop the relationship to make up for our heart's missing tendencies, but when we start to have problems with our own tendencies, we look around and suddenly the same-sex relationships aren't the way they used to be. Don't let that happen. Put your relationships with the same sex over those with the opposite sex. Give your "buds" of your own gender priority. Work on developing same-sex relationships while maintaining lower-priority but helpful opposite-sex relationships.

2) We put a specific member of the opposite sex in charge of "completing" us. This one even sounds dangerous. It actually sounds a bit like marriage. But it happens. Sometimes we do it without the other person knowing it. The answer isn't just about having a multitude of opposite-sex relationships. Not at all. We have to allow Christ some room to use people as He pleases. So what I mean to say is: Don't single somebody out.

Remember what I said? I said it kind of looks like marriage. We're teenagers. When we single somebody out, we're saying, *I think I found the person who can complete me, so I don't need my other friends.* I'm not saying you have to spend an equal amount of time with all your friends of the opposite sex. What I am saying is to be open to God using anyone of the opposite sex. It's okay to go with the flow if you're trusting God and obeying Him. A good way to do this is to spend time with members of the opposite sex who you respect but aren't close friends with. Maybe even spend time with the opposite sex of your family. By doing this, we can keep our eyes focused on the goal: to share in the fullness of God's heart.

3) We become dependent on a member of the opposite sex to meet one or more of our lifetime needs. You're asking, *What does this have to do with our different tendencies?* Let's say there's a guy in need of love and

affection. Wouldn't it be convenient for him to befriend a girl who has a tendency towards such love? I'm not saying he would do this on purpose. On the contrary, I believe he would befriend her simply for the balance of masculine and feminine. But if the situation were that this guy had not filled his need for love and affection with the living water, he would be very vulnerable in seeking balance from this girl. As he aims solely to seek a feminine influence, he will begin to soak up more of her than necessary because of his void. If the void had been filled, he would not be at risk of using her. As the relationship grows, he will become dependent on her for his needs.

This could also apply to a girl looking for, let's say, security. She could start depending on a guy to fill this void. This can apply to any of a person's needs. The key is to have the void filled before we start relationships with the opposite sex. Let's not make excuses when we notice these things start to happen. We need to call it like it is. If we don't, things can only get worse.

Disguised Addiction

We have a void; a need we haven't filled with the living water for whatever reason. Not only do we have a void, but we're also attracted to the opposite sex. If it just so happens our need is one of the tendencies of the opposite sex, which it most likely is, we're in serious danger. We're in even more danger if we keep heading towards that relationship.

In that case, we're growing closer to a member of the opposite sex who can "satisfy" our need. As we keep moving in that direction, we become more and more convinced that the relationship is what we need. We are kind of right, but we're mostly wrong. We're right because we need that masculine or feminine influence. We're wrong because that lifetime need should have been satisfied before we even considered the influence of the opposite sex.

I hope you're beginning to understand what's going on. There's massive confusion in our hearts. We know we need the influence. We also know we need our void filled. The influence is attracting us because it is what we're missing. But we're really missing the true source.

Remember what started this whole thing? We took our eyes off our Guide and Savior, Jesus Christ. We got distracted, and we started heading in the wrong direction. We forgot about the living water that never leaves us thirsty, and we instead turned to the earthly source that will always leave us thirsty. We're just mega confused.

The whole opposite sex thing makes it even more confusing. Like I mentioned before, this becomes an addiction. When we're addicted to a member of the opposite sex, we have a real issue. I think you could brainstorm a list of things that could happen. The other person has no clue what's happening, but do we ever stop to think what's happening to their heart? Do we ever consider the scars we're leaving behind? No, we don't. We're too focused on ourselves. We're too worried about our own needs. The deeper we get, the further we have to crawl out. It's like quicksand: the more we struggle, the more we sink. Who would guess that the next step would be to stay completely still?

We've Only Lost Sight

This section marks the end of focusing on our problem. Before we move on, I want to give you just a glimpse of hope. Remember when I asked you who was powerful enough to meet your needs all the time? Well, there is somebody. You'll never see Him if you stay headed in the wrong direction. In fact, if you're even facing the wrong direction, you'll never see His face. You once were following Him. You may not remember what He looks like. You may not remember His name. Do you remember His voice? It's been a long time.

Now, you're in the quicksand. If you've been shouting for help or yelling in frustration, or weeping in despair or moaning in pain, then I'd bet you haven't heard His voice. It's not because you've taken a wrong turn that you can't hear. Your ears can hear what's behind you unlike the sight of your eyes. I'll tell you why you can't hear. It's because you won't shut up. Be still. I'm telling you. I'm letting you know that He's telling you right now. Be still. His voice is like a whisper (I Kings 19:12-13). Be silent or call out to Him and be still. Listen for His voice. Then turn your eyes and look upon your Savior.

74 Love Is Here: A Teenager's Call to (Outstretched) Arms

Part Four: **THE PAIN**

X. Seeking The Truth

You probably looked at the title of part four and felt a little betrayed. *Zach, I thought you said we were finished with the problem. I thought you were gonna talk about the hope.* In our case, there's a unique connection between suffering and hope. The hope we have is in true love. We often reject our only hope because it's not attractive. In fact, this true love looks and feels a lot like suffering. I would say many of us aren't big fans of pain. It goes deeper than that.

I want you to understand four terms: earthly pain, earthly comfort, eternal pain, and eternal comfort. Earthly pain can be physical, emotional, or mental. Feeling "bad" in any of these areas is earthly pain. Likewise, earthly comfort is feeling "good" mentally, emotionally, or physically. I feel like we understand those pretty well. We experience earthly pain and comfort daily.

Eternal pain is spiritual. It is separation from God. Likewise, eternal comfort is intimacy with God. We can begin to experience eternal pain and comfort now, but it really sets in when we depart from this world. Where we put our faith now determines if we will experience eternal pain or eternal comfort when we die. The thing that strikes me is that eternal comfort often feels like earthly pain while we are living (I Corinthians 4:11). In the same way, eternal pain often feels like earthly comfort. Now, I'm not saying that this relationship exists after death. I believe we interpret these feelings this way because of our imperfection. When we die, we leave these earthly bodies behind. As we leave our earthly bodies, earthly pain and earthly comfort cease to exist.

So why am I telling you this? Because I know that our only hope looks and feels a lot like earthly pain, and if we choose to reject true love for that reason, we will never experience eternal comfort.

The Last Resort

I feel like many of us often turn to God only after we've exhausted all our other options. In the end, God turns out to be our last resort. I don't want to paint a picture in your mind of a God who doesn't accept you or only bitterly accepts you when you turn to Him as a last resort. God rejoices whenever you turn to Him. The Good Shepherd leaves the ninety-nine to go after the one (Matthew 18:12).

Remember the prodigal son? He took his dad's money, went out and threw wild parties, lost all the money, and became ragged and homeless. We've all been in that position. Maybe you're there now. We've exhausted all our options, and we've turned up completely empty. We're naked and shameful, but what did the prodigal son do? He turned around one day, looked down the path he had taken, remembered when he made the wrong turn and headed down the road of destruction, and he started walking home. What did his dad do when he saw him in the distance? He ran to him, embraced him and kissed him, immediately put a ring on his finger and a fine robe on his back, and called him "Son". His dad then threw a party for him, welcoming him home.

Christ isn't gonna treat us differently if He's our last resort. He loves us so much that He's going to accept us back by pouring out all His good things on us. God may be your last resort, but you are His first priority.

So do you remember what was happening to us? We were sinking in the quicksand of the relationship we thought would satisfy our needs. Then we became still so we could hear His voice. When we had been still for so long we could've given up, we heard His whisper to us. So we turned around, and now what do we see? We see Jesus standing in front of us, in front of the quicksand, His arms outstretched to us. In His arms is a cross. He's holding the cross out to us, above the quicksand. We don't know what to do, so we listen to His voice. We finally understand His whisper, *Take hold of my cross*. Here comes decision time. We recognize the cross. We know it symbolizes His love poured out for us. We also know it symbolizes earthly pain and suffering. We know true love, His love, is our only hope of getting out of the quicksand, but we're afraid of the pain we will feel when we grab hold of it. There will be pain, but it's a lot better than sinking in the quicksand.

Make the decision to take hold of the cross. Respond to Jesus, *Yes, Lord*. He will pull you out of whatever situation you're stuck in. He is the hope. Trust Him with your life.

Finding Our Best Friend

Earlier, I mentioned that Jesus can be your best friend. *So if I want Him to be my best friend, what exactly would that look like?*

A necessary part of it is spending time with Him. To me, this includes giving Him the majority of our thoughts. Out of everyone, we should think about Him the most.

We must also give Him the majority of our communication. This includes prayer, both casually and formally, time reading the Bible, His Word, and meditation in stillness. We don't do it because we have to, we do it because we desire to be with Him.

Finally, we must give Him control of our actions and behavior. Before everything we say and do, we must decide if it will honor God. Every word and every moment, every breath either praises God or not. When our Savior becomes our best friend, every breath becomes a precious sacrifice to Him.

Before we move on, I want to make sure you understand something. That cross that Christ rescued us with, we don't leave it behind when we choose to walk with Christ again. Once we're saved, He says something after "take hold of my cross". He now says, *Take up your cross and follow me.* Our first response probably isn't, *Yay, God! Let's get to it!* We wouldn't be human if we responded that way. We hesitate to take up the cross and carry it as we walk with Christ. Honestly, a cross is pretty heavy. It seems impossible to lift, let alone carry it for a lifetime. Yet Jesus calls this burden "light" (Matthew 11:30). How can that be?

The answer is in the power of Christ. Humanly speaking, the cross is unbearable, but "I can do everything through Christ, who gives me strength" (Philippians 4:13). Without Christ, we'd crumple under the weight of the cross. But He's right beside us and inside us. This doesn't eliminate the burden. Christ simply enables us to handle the burden.

So what is the burden? It's the pain that accompanies holy and righteous living. When we follow Christ, we have to say no to many things. There are many temptations that we must run from. I've said it before, and I'll say it again: the media is downright dirty. We must separate from anything--movies, music, books, games, shows, etc.--that is not pleasing to God (Ephesians 5:10). If it would not please God, it has no place in your life. Throw it out. Even worldly things *that we value* we must discard. There's pain in this. People may treat us differently, but that is the burden of your cross (I Peter 4:4). He'll give you the strength to make it. Follow Him daily, and with your cross as a reminder of your previous state, make Him your best friend.

His Love Has No Limits

So far, I've only explained our side of the Jesus-is-my-best-friend relationship. I've only talked about our sacrifice. It's true, our sacrifice is necessary to a relationship with Christ, but that's only half of it. As we choose to walk with Jesus, we begin to receive from Him. We give Christ our lives, He gives us His love. This is something to get excited about.

Remember, when I first mentioned our lifetime needs I explained that we often make bad decisions when choosing the sources to fill those needs. I explained that any worldly source including relationships couldn't bring true satisfaction. What we get is temporary satisfaction; satisfaction from an outside source. This often results in addiction. We start depending on an outside source for satisfying our needs. Then we learned that the only source of true satisfaction is Jesus. We learned about the living water. Christ specifically says that this water turns into a spring in our hearts. That's why we never thirst again. The source is inside of us. The satisfaction of our lifetime needs is constantly renewed inside our hearts when we choose to accept the living water Christ offers us.

Are you as amazed as I am? This is a good reason to be thankful to God. *Zach, I'm a little confused. You're going too fast. Can you please slow it down for me?* I'm sorry. I'll take a step back.

We're teenagers. We've decided to give our hearts to Christ. We are now children of God. We have chosen to shine the light Christ has given us in our dark society. We are devoted to loving others and making disciples of our fellow teenagers. We were following Christ, but we took our eyes off Him. We thought we found a better source to fill our needs but really, it only took us further from our Guide. When we were ready to give up, Christ called out to us. We turned to Him, and He lifted us out of our difficult situation. We are now following Him again, ready to suffer for His sake. He is our best friend. We have begun to give Him ourselves and in doing so, He has revealed to us His living water. This water will reside in our hearts, satisfying our needs at the core. In this way, it is easier to keep our eyes on Him. Christ says we will never thirst again.

So what is this living water? Well, it's not something you can take without being offered. It is a gift from Christ. So how do we receive it? We receive it when we truly give Him our hearts. When we are surrendered to Christ, then and only then can our needs be truly satisfied. What does it mean to be surrendered? It means that we're living for Christ all the time. Or even better, Christ is working through us all the time. If we're doing our own thing, we're not surrendered. If we're drinking, smoking, cussing, telling dirty jokes or laughing at them, gossiping, engaging in sexual immorality, encouraging sin, being lazy, being prideful, being jealous, hurting someone, judging someone, leading someone on, getting into a relationship we know we shouldn't, flirting, the list goes on and on; if we are letting sin control us, we are not surrendered. We must be dead to sin for us to have surrendered our hearts. It's not easy.

Be honest with yourself. I was in that place not too long ago. I still struggle with it. That's the thing though. We can be Christians and never drink the living water. When you accept Christ as your Savior, He places this faucet in your heart. The faucet is running with living water. We can choose to open the valve or close the valve at any moment. Some Christians never open it. If we are surrendered, the valve is open and the living water is satisfying our needs. If we are doing our own thing, the valve is closed, and we are not experiencing true satisfaction of our needs.

Every moment we must choose to open or close the valve by either surrendering to Christ or not. If you want true satisfaction, surrender every moment, and the living water will never run dry. It's a weird feeling to be satisfied from the inside, but it feels real good, and it's available to you every second of every day for the rest of life. Drink up!

He Shows Off

Okay, so let's say we're doing it. We are surrendering every moment, and amidst the heartache, we are feeling deep satisfaction from the flow of the living water. *What kind of forward progress am I making by doing this? What exactly can God do with my life?* A surrendered heart is a beautiful thing. I still don't understand why I feel the way I do when I live for Christ, but I'm gonna try to put it into words.

When we are living for Christ, we are fulfilling our mission. Yes, sometimes it hurts, but the joy that comes from living out our purpose on this planet is incredible. Our hearts belong to Christ, and when He's in possession, we get a taste of fulfillment. When we're drinking the living water, Christ becomes clear and everything else grows dim. If you've tasted this water, you know what I'm talking about. You see the world for what it is, and your eyes become very sensitive to the love that surrounds you. It's basically a high. It's like getting drunk on the living water, and it's awesome. It's a taste of life without sin.

You know you've drunk the living water when you've disappeared to yourself, and all that remains is loving those around you as Christ would. We don't always have the pleasure of experiencing this level of oneness with Christ. At times, we even feel distant. We must surrender our hearts. What Christ can do is unbelievable, literally. It's something to be thankful for.

XI. Accepting The Truth

As we return to Christ, we must do something alongside surrendering and drinking the living water. It is what most would call "learning from our mistakes". Christ shows us what we did wrong as we walk with Him. He does this for our benefit. He doesn't want us to get distracted again, so He allows us to see where we took that wrong turn. I find it amusing how clear our mistakes become once we turn to Christ. The fact is that everything becomes clearer. When we've gone wrong in relationships, it's especially important to learn how we got there and what the consequences of that mistake were. It's important because we're dealing not only with ourselves but also with other people. Our mistake can really screw somebody else up and get that person in as much sin as ourselves. So we need to learn. We need to understand the moves we made so we can have some method of prevention. If we want to love others, we need to learn from our screwed up relationships.

Misguided Love

So what went wrong? It's not that you stopped loving the specific person. You were made to love. It's what we do. It's what we're supposed to be all about: selfless, Christ-like love. We've got this down. So we started loving this person, and everything was good and normal for awhile. But the moment that love stopped being about Christ, it became misguided, unfruitful, and even harmful. What were the symptoms of that? Apparently, they were undetectable at the time. But in all seriousness, loving became personal.

Love is pointing others to Christ through our actions and words. Love isn't a feeling that you can give someone or that you can get from someone. No, love is a lifestyle. What does it look like? It looks exactly like the life of Christ. He is love. Imitating Christ is love. There's no bending it into your personal version of love. Misguided love is doing it our way. If you're doing something Christ wouldn't do, it's not love. You don't give love. You live love. The biggest mistake we can make is to confuse salvation and love. Christ says to love each other *as I have loved you.* We think, *Oh! Christ saved me from my sin by reaching into my heart and getting intimate with me. If I want to imitate Him and obey Him, I have to do the same to my friends.* That's not love. That's salvation. You don't have the power to save your friend from sin. Christ gives salvation. We can't. We point to Him. We lead our friends to Him, but we don't try to save them. Instead, we love each other by the way we live.

Our love is misguided when we think we can make a difference in someone's heart. You are called to live a life of love to everyone around you. Christ will make the difference in your friend's life. Don't stand in the way of that. Later, we're gonna talk about how to love in this way. For now, just remember that it's not something we can give, it's the way we live. When we try to make others feel "our love", we actually just stand in the way of Christ's true love. Learn from that mistake. Let's stop hurting our friends by loving them our way. Let's start to live love.

We Were Ignorant

When we reflect upon the mistake that we've made, we usually find ourselves saying, *I just didn't know what I was getting into. If I would've known, I wouldn't have done it.* Christ reveals our ignorance. Then we're saying we wish somebody would have stopped us. Personally, I don't think it would have mattered. We weren't just ignorant, we were arrogant. We would have said, *I know what I'm doing.* So how do we learn from that mistake? The solution isn't an easy one.

The problem is that we're not open to a change in our relationship. At that point, it hasn't gotten bad enough for us to be open to change. So my advice is this: always be open to God interrupting your comfortable life. In fact, be open to Him turning your life upside down. This attitude will make the difference. The longer we remain stubborn, regardless of our circumstances, the more we hurt ourselves. A stubborn heart leads to a sick heart. Stubborn is another word for closed, and if our hearts are closed, Jesus can't make things better.

Whether you think you're right or not, allow God to prove you wrong. Try to defend your case before God, but allow Him to do His part too. Being stubborn isn't cool. Take your case to God and be ready for Him to turn your world upside down. The longer you remain stubborn, the longer you remain in ignorance, and the longer you torture yourself, rejecting the Healer, Himself.

We Rejected Him

Rejection. I'm not too fond of it. I'm guessing you feel the same way. When we reject someone, we're saying, *You're not important.* When we do our own thing, we reject God. We tell Him, *You're not important.* This is the God of the universe. He's our Guide and the source of living water. Yet we reject Him for our own ways. It's sad that as children of God, we do this all the time. If we truly loved Him, we would do His thing. On a daily basis, we damage our relationship with God. What's going on here? What's our problem? If we love Him, it should be our pleasure to give up our ways for His. Instead, we reject the one we love.

Obviously, this is a terrible mistake. As we walk with Christ after He rescues us we see the pain we made Him endure. He reveals to us just how badly we mocked Him with choosing our own ways. How do we learn from this? From now on, we are aware of the pain in our actions. We are aware that we hurt God by living for ourselves. So let's stop doing it. Let's choose His way because we love Him.

We Now Know

The pain is evident. When we take our eyes off Christ, our love hurts others, ourselves, and our Savior. Maybe you're reading this and you haven't experienced that pain in your life. Maybe you haven't made these mistakes. Good, learn from them. The truth is that most of us have caused this pain. Today, we're either in the midst of it or looking back on it. Christ has revealed to us the truth of our mistakes. He's shown us the path we took to screw up, and He's shown us the consequences of our actions.

This marks the end of talking about the past. We now know what our mistakes were. We're ready to change and make sure we don't mess up again. We are passionate about loving the right way. We know we were meant to love, and we know misguided love is dangerous. Now we are eager to live love. This is the lifestyle we've been called to. We've learned from our mistakes. Now we're ready to turn around, get back on track, and run towards the finish line. We've set our eyes back on Christ. He is our Guide. The future looks promising. But we need one final weapon before we enter into battle once again. We need one more piece of understanding. Then we're off.

XII. The Truth Has Set Us Free

Remember when we were stuck in the quicksand? We were deep in sin. We were sinking when we heard the voice of truth. We then began to seek out the truth. As a result, we found our best friend, Jesus Christ. He healed us as we began to surrender to Him and drink the living water He offered. He revealed the truth of our sin to us, and we had to accept the truth that we caused hurt by going our own way. He taught us in this way so that we wouldn't do it again. There's one final step. We need to act out in love. But that's the thing. We need to know how to truly love. Now's the time for the truth to set us free. Now's the time for God to take our pain, the hurt we caused, and mold it into love, our new perfect and pleasing lifestyle.

Love Is Selfless

Love is a lifestyle of selflessness. That means we can't aim to please ourselves and love at the same time. If we're asking ourselves questions like, *What will I get out of this? What does this person have to offer me? What will people think of me? Is this going to make me feel uncomfortable?*, then we are being selfish. We are focused on ourselves more than we think we are. We should be asking questions like, *Is what I'm doing honoring to God? Is this something Jesus would do? Will my actions or the words I speak point this person to Christ or myself? If I refrain from saying this, will this person be held back from experiencing more of God?* You see, these thoughts are focused on how our actions will affect someone's relationship with Christ. Love encourages movement towards Christ not each other. *Who am I encouraging movement towards? Does my life attract people to myself or to my faith?*

We get so caught up in trying to look the best in each others' eyes that we forget what we look like to Christ. Sometimes we don't care. That is selfishness. A life of selfishness is a spotlight on yourself. A life of love is a spotlight on your Savior. Your thoughts and behavior are either a spotlight on you or God. Where's the spotlight pointed? Let's start delighting in taking the attention off ourselves and placing it on Jesus Christ.

Love Does Not Hold Expectations

Our lifestyle of love forbids placing expectations on our relationships to fill any of our lifetime needs. Expectations like these are deadly to loving relationships because they take the focus off Christ. His living water is supposed to fill our needs. If we start thinking a specific person is the source of this satisfaction, we need to take our eyes off that person and place them on Jesus. Love never expects satisfaction from anyone but

Jesus, and love never accepts satisfaction from anyone but Jesus. Relationships can only be loving when the focus is entirely on Jesus. We need to place our expectations on our Guide, our Heavenly Father.

Please understand me, now. Expectations inside of our relationships are good and necessary. We must expect our brothers and sisters in Christ to obey His commands and live by His Word. In this way, we can encourage one another. In this way, our relationships on earth can make a difference in eternity. If you connect the dots, you see this only happens when our focus is entirely on Christ. Bottom-line: Your expectations will always lie on the one you focus on. Therefore, Christ must be your Guide as you live love.

Love Does Not Fill Another's Spiritual Needs

This section may be difficult for you to read. That's not because I think you're stupid. It's because this is just life. It can be confusing. We don't always understand everything. So what I want to say is this: Love does not meet the spiritual needs of a friend. When we see someone who is desiring satisfaction of the spirit, our initial reaction is to do all that we can to satisfy that person. *I mean, if we really loved them, wouldn't we try to satisfy them?* Our love is only a reflection of God. Our love points our friends to Christ. Through Christ, they receive the living water and are satisfied. We have to quit thinking love is supposed to meet these needs. It's not! Love is pointing people to Christ through our behavior. That's it. That's all it is. We do that, and the rest is up to Christ. This lifestyle does not meet the spiritual needs of others. That wouldn't be an accomplishment, because we can't save people from sin. Through this lifestyle, Jesus claims individual hearts. When people see Him in us, they seek Him out, and they find what they've been searching for. And it's not found in you. It's found in Jesus Christ. He will reveal His love through your life. Remember, we make disciples. We don't lead people to ourselves, we lead people to Christ.

I say "spiritual needs" because there are other needs that we *are* called to meet. Spiritual needs are met through the living water and thus can only be met by God. These "other needs" are the temporary needs that humans can meet. As the hands and feet of Christ, we love by meeting the urgent needs of "the least" (Titus 3:14, Matthew 25:40). Our lifetime needs are both "urgent" and "spiritual" because our love can temporarily meet the need to an extent, but God can meet the need for eternity in full. God has given us the ability to express His goodness only in part because He wants us to depend upon Him. Nevertheless, He wants us to express this goodness towards others as best we can.

Love Reflects The Truth

Okay, so we know that a true lifestyle of love will point people to Christ. How? Well, I won't to go into too much detail at this moment, but I do want to give you the gist of it. Our lives, our behavior should reflect the truth every moment. *Okay, so what's the truth?* Well, it can be ugly. The truth is what Christ has done for us. It is our sin and how He saved us from it. The truth is that sin has consequences and Christians face suffering. The truth can be summed up in the image of the cross. It's pain, yet it's our only source of hope and comfort. Therefore, love should reflect hope, comfort, and pain. We suffer when we turn our back on this world. Our friends need to see this. They shouldn't see a sugar-coated version of love. We're giving it to them raw. There's pain in love, in our new lifestyle. But there's also hope.

We look to a brighter future. We look past this earth and into eternity. We base our behavior on eternal value, our possessions on eternal value, and our thoughts and ideas on eternal value. Our hope is in eternity (Philippians 3:20). That is made clear through love.

Finally, we reflect comfort. We are at peace because God has a plan for our lives. We've put our worries on Him (Psalm 23:4; John 14:27; John 16:33). We know Him to be the solution to our difficulties. We know we are His first priority. He is watching over us every moment. We know we can always rest in His embrace. This we reflect through love. This is the truth of the cross. We are saved, and it is apparent in our lives. This is what Jesus has done and what the world will see, and they will turn to Him.

Love Is Here: A Teenager's Call to (Outstretched) Arms

Part Five: **THE PURPOSE**

98 Love Is Here: A Teenager's Call to (Outstretched) Arms

XIII. Teenagers Are Made To Love…

It's time to think back now. Remember what got us to this place. We accepted Christ into our hearts to fix our sin problem and dwell inside of us. We learned that our hearts were made to love. So we tried to love. We tried to love those around us. We tried to lead the blind to Christ. We tried to be a light in our dark society. Somewhere along the way, we got distracted. We took our eyes off our Savior, Jesus Christ. As a result, we wandered back into darkness. We were reunited with hurt. But in our deepest and darkest place, the Shepherd called to us. We responded, and His cross saved us once again. Since then, we've come to know Christ as our best friend. He's shown us a glimpse of His love. It's the life He has called us to live as teenagers.

We know that love is selfless, that love does not place personal expectations on people except those that are biblical, that love does not satisfy the spiritual needs of others, and that love always reflects the truth, always leading people to Christ. Now we must apply this to our lives. We must actually begin to live it. But, of course, you say, *Zach, I'm not convinced yet. I need more information on this lifestyle so I can feel more prepared.* In that case, I first want to make the pie crust of love. Without the crust, we wouldn't know the pie was a pie. The filling is important because it provides the specific pie flavor but the crust holds the pie together. In this chapter, I want to create this crust step by step. In the end, we will know that the pie is going to be a pie, and that love is going to be true love.

By The Power of Christ Alone

The first element of the structure of love is the source that provides the ability to live such a lifestyle. The source, as you probably guessed, is Christ. He was, and will forever be, the standard of love. We need what He had. What He had came from God. What He had was the Holy Spirit. The Holy Spirit lives inside all believers. The Holy Spirit is God's gift to all who put their faith in Jesus. Engaging the Spirit is the only way to utilize the power of Christ. This power is available to us if we desire it. This power comes from being in tune with the Holy Spirit. This power is not only an important element of love, but it's also the only tool that will ever be able to create true love.

In the next chapter, I'm going to get specific in ways to love people. For now, you have to know that the Holy Spirit is the only way we can actually love at all. Our actions, words, and thoughts need to come from somewhere. There are two options, you can either let the enemy produce your actions, words, and thoughts, or you can let God through His Holy

Spirit produce them in you. You say, *But I choose what I say, think, and act. It's not Satan or God.* If God isn't controlling your behavior, the evil one has control. When we surrender to God, we decide to listen and obey His voice, the Holy Spirit. The more time we spend with God in His Word, in prayer, and in meditation, the more familiar we become with His voice. When He speaks, we must obey. In this way, we can truly live love, and His is the only way. Many have tried to find other, easier ways. Let me tell you right now that no other way works. We must obey the Lord at all costs.

In Harmony With One Another

The first ingredient of our pie crust was the source of the power to love that is in Christ. The second is the element of coming together as brothers and sisters to love alongside each other. This is crucial to successful love. We need people to commit to the same lifestyle as us. We need these people so that we can encourage each other and relate to each other. These mutual relationships are necessary. We need to push each other and hold each other accountable. If you try to love on your own, you're gonna fail. We need each other specifically for this. So let's partner with other Christians.

Some of us don't like this idea. We aren't too sure about coming alongside the Christians we know. It's one of those situations where we think we'd be better off alone. We won't. It doesn't work that way with love. You say, *Jesus died alone. None of His followers went to the cross with Him.* You're right. Isn't that a shame? Don't be like those guys. Stand by your Christian friends. Don't let them do it alone. The truth is our Christian friends may do to us like Jesus' followers did to Him. We may end up alone at times. People may desert us. When that happens, we must still carry out God's will by obeying Him. Jesus made the choice to surround Himself with followers. That's what He was about. He didn't want to die alone, but He had to. We must follow the example of Jesus by surrounding ourselves with people who also desire to live love.

We have to remember, Jesus didn't forget about the disciples when they deserted Him. He came back to them three days later and forgave them. You have no excuse to do it alone. We are called to love alongside our brothers and sisters. Let's stop avoiding them, and let's start utilizing those relationships to further Christ's Kingdom.

To Reflect The Love Of Christ

The third element is one you're probably tired of hearing me say. It's the fact that we must reflect Christ. We are commanded to imitate Christ in everything we do. People need to look at us and see Jesus. Plain and simple. How do we do this? We must let go of ourselves.

The world tells us to hold onto our independence. As children of God committed to love, we need to eagerly surrender our independence to God with joyful hearts. We lose ourselves, and God fills us with the Spirit. Then He is able to work through us, so we can truly live the life of love He has called us to. This is our sole purpose: to reflect Christ in all that we do. This is love. It's the same thing. If we can get love right, then we don't need anything else. It is true that all you need is love. Not only is it all we need, but it's the only thing we should focus on. Our focus should always be on imitating Christ in everything we do, so that we will live every moment in love. This is what it means to be in love with Jesus.

We've surrendered ourselves to Him, and we are reflecting Him through our behavior. Don't let anyone convince you that love is something other than this. Jesus is love because He lived a sinless life (I John 2:8). Therefore, when we imitate Him, in that moment, we are in love. Can you imagine how it must feel to fall in love? When this happens, you won't be able to keep from imitating Christ. When this happens, we will be fully surrendered to Him.

To The World

The final step is understanding to whom we reflect Christ. The answer is simple. We must reflect Christ to everyone around us. Honestly, this isn't something we should have to worry about. If we are truly living love, everyone around us will have to notice it. What does this mean to us? It means that Christ didn't love some people and not love others (James 2:9). He wasn't two-faced. We must follow this example. Everyone around us should see Christ in us. If some people see Christ and others don't, then we're not really loving. Remember, love isn't something you can give to people. Love is a lifestyle. Therefore, anyone who turns up in our lives should see Christ in us. If you're surrendered to Christ, you will live the same at home, at school, at church, and anywhere else you go. This is how love is supposed to work. We can't personalize it. It's already been personalized by Christ, and we all must follow His model.

Love Is Here: A Teenager's Call to (Outstretched) Arms

XIV. The Foundation For Life

We understand the pie crust of love. Now it's time to examine the filling. This is the true substance. This is the tasty stuff. Here we start to get practical. I want to show you some specific ways we can imitate Christ. We need to *really* pay attention to this, because when it comes down to it, how we live every moment determines if we're truly loving. Every moment counts for eternity. We have to be continually living a life of love, not just during certain moments. We need to love even when no one is watching. God records all of our actions. Therefore, we must always act in love. This is a decision we must make every moment. There's always the option to live for yourself and do your own thing. But we need to choose to surrender our actions and thoughts to Christ every moment. Living love doesn't happen without effort. It takes energy to love. It takes discipline to devote every breath to imitating Christ. We need to make the effort. It will be well worth it (Hebrews 12:11).

Love By Sacrifice

Love requires sacrifice. In fact, we are meant to be a living sacrifice (Romans 12:1). I know this doesn't make love sound very appealing. Especially as teenagers. I'm not sure we usually get pumped about sacrificing ourselves. But if we are to love, we need to be a living sacrifice.

So what does that look like? When I say sacrifice, I mean we are to give something over to Christ. Therefore, a living sacrifice gives everything to Christ all the time. What is everything? I would say time, talents, treasure, trials and triumphs, and thoughts both inwardly and outwardly expressed through behavior. That pretty much covers everything. I know you're probably thinking, *Wow, I'm not sure I can handle sacrificing even one of those.* I know it's overwhelming. All at once, it's hard to think of sacrificing those things. We must, however, give it all to God. It starts with the *desire* to sacrifice everything to our Savior. It's a lot easier when our hearts are in the right place. So I once again remind you to surrender completely to Christ.

Our time. Are we giving God our time? Are we taking time to read the Bible everyday? Are we taking time to pray passionately everyday? Are we taking time to simply listen for God's voice without distraction everyday? I'm using the phrase, "taking time", but the truth is that we probably need to take some time from doing our own things so we can actually get these other things done. That is sacrifice. We take time from our own things, and we devote that time to scripture reading, praying, and silence before God. This is part of living love. There are no excuses for not giving God our time. We also need to sacrifice time for service to God. This can be at church or anywhere, but we need to be taking time out of our normal routine to serve the Lord.

Our talents. We are all gifted in some area. We can either use this gift to further some earthly agenda or to give glory to God's name. So I'm proposing that we use our gifts to glorify God. No matter what they are, no matter what you're good at, just ask God to help you use it to further His Kingdom. Surrender your talents to God in that way. That is sacrifice. We use our talents to lift up God, not ourselves.

Our treasure. God has entrusted us with material possessions. I'm not here to tell you how to use your possessions for God and not yourself. But I am here to tell you that they must be used and devoted to Christ's Kingdom. We once again must ask God to show us how to accomplish this. We must trust that He will show us. Our possessions belong to God; let's use them to lift Him up.

Our trials and triumphs. God has a plan for our lives. We are going to experience a variety of trials and triumphs. We sacrifice these to God by praising Him though the thick and the thin. We listen to His voice in our highs and lows. We allow Him to change us through all our circumstances. We accept that they are the result of His good plan for our lives. Therefore, we trust Him, give Him the glory, and take no pride for ourselves.

Our thoughts. These are the hardest to sacrifice because we must do it without ceasing. How do we do it? Well, we have to do something that seems a bit redundant. We have to think about what we think. What I mean is that we need to take every thought captive (II Corinthians 10:5). If it doesn't please the Lord, we think no more about it. If it does please Him, we continue to think about it. You'd be surprised at how many thoughts come into our minds that do not please the Lord. I'm telling you there are *a lot*. We have to throw them out with passion. Even the ones we think are okay. If they do not obviously please the Lord, get rid of them. We must sacrifice our thoughts. As we clean out the sinful thoughts, we replace them with pure, focused thoughts on the Lord (Philippians 4:8). I want to challenge you to revolutionize your thought life. Let's start thinking about Jesus. He deserves our daydreaming time. I know that you will find these thoughts much more satisfying than the old ones.

What happens if we don't do this? It turns out that our thoughts influence our behavior. If we dwell on sinful thoughts, then our words and actions will be sinful. On the other hand, if we dwell on pure thoughts that come from the Holy Spirit, our actions and words will reflect that purity (Romans 8:6).

Isn't that what love is all about? We surrender these things; we sacrifice ourselves so that we may reflect Christ, which in itself is love. Remember, we are a living sacrifice. Every moment we sacrifice ourselves to Christ. He works though us, people see Him, and Christ's Kingdom advances, all because teenagers decided they would sacrifice themselves to Christ.

Love By Grace

Okay, so we understand sacrifice. We know we need to give Christ everything every moment. We know that's necessary for love. But what about when we're around other people? We all know that certain people make it a lot harder for us to love. How do we imitate Christ then? It's called grace. We talk a lot about it when referring to Jesus, so it's probably important to understand it.

What is grace? Grace is showing somebody love when they don't deserve it. It's what Jesus did for us on the cross. He died for our sins, not when we had it all together, but when we were living in sin and loving it (Romans 5:8). He died for us when we were sinners, yet we find it hard to be kind to those who aren't. We need to show grace.

We all know the feeling, *This person keeps pushing me and pushing me. It's impossible to be like Jesus when I'm around this person.* We feel that way because we don't have grace. Lots of us picture grace as this beautiful gift that makes everyone happy. The truth is that grace can be ugly. We humble ourselves by showing Christ's love to someone who irritates us and most often, we don't get anything for it (II Corinthians 12:15). We are even mocked for it. Grace doesn't result in happy feelings, but it displays an accurate reflection of Christ.

Remember, our job isn't to save people. Christ will do the saving. Our job is to reflect Christ. We can do this through grace. We most often won't see results, but it's the right thing to do regardless of the results.

Humility and grace are a package deal. You can't show grace through pride. For grace to shine through, we have to tear down our pride so that only humility remains. When we show grace, we wash the sinner's feet. It's a humble position, but it's the position of Christ. When you see an opportunity to show grace, eagerly do it. This is one of the best ways to imitate Christ. If we want to truly love, we need to become fountains of grace for all people to drink from.

Love By Peace

We are called to live in peace with one another (Romans 12:18). This includes believers as well as those who don't believe. We are not to treat people harshly. We are to be at peace with our neighbor. Think of a peaceful person. Does that person treat others worse than himself? If someone is truly at peace with others, God, and self, Christ's love will pour out of that person. Sin creates the opposite of peace. Sin results in turmoil. Therefore, peace is being free from the power of sin. When someone dies, we say, "rest in peace". When someone dies to sin, we can say the same thing. We are free from turmoil when we truly die to sin and to our flesh.

What I'm trying to say is that if we are gonna love by peace, we need to die to our sinful nature (Romans 6:11). Everyday is a battle against the flesh. But Christ gives us victory over the flesh everyday. It is up to us to choose to die to our flesh in every moment. This results in peace. Our peace will be visible to the world, and people will see Christ in us. This peace will cover our relationships to people, to ourselves, and to God. We need it, and we need it to last. Therefore, we need to die to our flesh whenever it tries to take over. Peace results from experiencing freedom from sin. The result of peace is a life of love. The result of a life of love is a reflection of Christ. The result of reflecting Christ is a larger Kingdom under His authority.

Love By Fellowship

The last aspect of love I want to talk about is definitely my favorite. It's called fellowship. It consists of Christians doing life together. How does this tie into love? Well, God doesn't simply call us to reflect Christ to unbelievers, He calls us to model Christ's love to each other. That's why we meet together as brothers and sisters. We want to encourage each other in our walks with Christ. It can be through words and discussion, but the truth is that the way we live around believers speaks louder than the words from our mouths (I John 3:18). When we "fellowship", we are encouraging each other either through words or actions or both.

It is the time for healing. Fellowship is a break from the world. It is kind of like half-time during a sports game. We're taking a break from the game to regroup, encourage, and refuel. It's a time to get our focus back on Christ.

I don't want to talk too much about what fellowship should look like. We just need to know that a life of love includes doing life with other believers to encourage each other spiritually. Without fellowship, our souls will dry up, our needs will resurface, and we will get distracted. God knows we need each other (1 Corinthians 12:21). Christ knows it. Let's get excited about fellowship. It's the definition of Church. True church is fellowship. Fellowship is a major part of love, so we must make it a major part of our lives.

XV. Get The Picture

For quite a while now, we've been narrowing in on love. We know it is a lifestyle. We know what it's about and how it's done. Now, I want to bring us back to where we started. I want you to see the big picture.

We're teenagers. Society doesn't want us to surrender to Christ because we have the potential to strike some hard blows against the enemy. Culture is attacking us. Sin is encouraged everywhere. It can seem overwhelming at times. Our friends think they are *good-for-nothing*. We know we are much more as children of God, but sometimes we feel *good-for-nothing*. We know we've been called. We've been selected to fight for Christ against the enemy. God gives us a special weapon. It's called *love*. It's a life that we must choose to live. As long as we are living love, we are doing all we can to fight the enemy. Whether we can see the results of not, we are winning the battle. Our goal is to die fighting. Not dying in an epic way like Boromir in *Lord of The Rings* or Nameless in *Hero*, we hope to die like the American soldiers on the beaches of Normandy. We long to die alongside our brothers and sisters. We are only given a lifetime to fight the enemy. Let's be ruthless in our love. Let's never hold back.

Why am I even talking about death? Because love is our life's purpose. From birth until death, we are complete in love. We were made to love. Yes, us. Teenagers. This is the big picture. I talked about getting distracted and taking our eyes off Jesus because I don't want us to fall into those traps. They hinder us from doing our duty as soldiers in Christ's Army. We have to stay focused as we fight. I hope you now understand more about your purpose and your design. I hope that God has opened your eyes to see and understand the image of true love. Obviously, this book isn't over yet. I still need to say a few more things. Just remember the culture you're facing. Remember why you're living for Christ. We desire to see change in the hearts of those around us. We desire to see sin powerless in our lives and our friends' lives. We desire to see the enemy crumble as we simply breathe love. That's our vision. That's why we are here.

John 15

Jesus says, *Remain in my love*. He goes on to say that if we obey His commandments, we remain in His love. What does that mean? It means that Christ tells us to do some things. If we obey Him, we will live the life of love. He takes this a step further when He says, *There is no greater love than to lay down one's life for a friend.* That's a powerful statement. So does Jesus expect us to die for our friends? The answer is: Yeah, He does. He meant what He said. *Did Jesus mean we are to physically die so our friends can physically live?* Maybe He did. It's possible that you will have the privilege to die in that way. I believe that regardless of how we physically die, Christ calls us to die to ourselves everyday. *If we die to ourselves and surrender to Christ, how does that allow our friends to live?* When we die to ourselves, we reflect the life of Christ. The life of Christ is the source of eternal life. Who knows? We might end up physically dying to save a friend. But Christ can save our friends as we daily die to ourselves.

Jesus also says that we didn't choose Him, He chose us. *What on earth does that mean?* God has a plan for us. We have no say in that plan. It's true, we've been given the freedom to choose. We have a thing called *freewill*. The thing is, God already knows the choices we're going to make. He created us to make those choices. So when we choose to give our lives to Jesus, we're merely carrying out His plan.

Many people think that we can do whatever we feel like because God's plan is always gonna work out. That's true. We can. But if that's what you're thinking, you're headed for destruction. Those that God has chosen are on a totally different playing field than those He hasn't (Romans 9:22-23). That doesn't mean God only calls the godly. No, God calls us to Him as filthy sinners. There are certain people that are headed for Hell, but we must understand that it's impossible for us to know who those people are. We all look the same. We have to give everyone an equal chance to turn to God, including ourselves. We can't say, *I must be one of those people that's headed to Hell*. If you're saying that right now, or you're not sure, I want you to know that God's calling you to Himself. You are being called to break free from sin and become a child of God.

He's chosen us. It's our job to tell everyone about the salvation Jesus offers (Colossians 1:28). We do that through living love. That's why Jesus then goes on to say, *This is my command: love each other*. This is our mission.

There are those out there who need to know they've been chosen. They won't know until they know love, until they see Christ in us. Jesus has created us, called us, and commanded us. It's time we accepted our design of love, followed our call to love, and obeyed our command to love.

Called To Love All The Time

Zach, I know we're supposed to love all the time. I know it's a lifestyle. I know every moment should be lived in love. But what does that have to do with the big picture? When we take that step back to get a broader view of our lives, we see that there are times when we're really excited and eager to love, but we also see that there are times when love is the last thing we want. There will be times when you don't feel like loving. But let me ask you something. When a pitcher doesn't feel like pitching, does he just not do it? Or how about when a teacher isn't in the mood to teach, does the teacher just not go to school? How about when a child of God doesn't feel like loving, does he take the day off? The answer is no.

Those people don't just stop what they're doing because they're not in the mood. They can't. Why? Because they have a responsibility to do what they've been called to do. There are no breaks for those that have been called to love. When we're not in the mood, we can't just stop. If we do stop, there are consequences. The pitcher may not pitch again. The teacher may not teach again. The child of God may not love again. The pattern is that when we disregard our responsibilities, they are taken away from us. When I say, *Love all the time,* I'm talking forward progress. I'm talking we get more and more responsibility as we love in every moment as opposed to less and less responsibility as we disregard our call to love (Matthew 25:29). Maybe you're saying, *Less responsibility sounds good for me.* I'd just ask you to remember that we live off love. This is how we get filled up. This is how we experience the living water. Do you really want God to take that away from you? You will never be satisfied unless you drink from the living water. All other water is temporary satisfaction. We need to accept our responsibility to love even when we don't feel like it. In this way, we will be filled. That's promised to us.

Your Heart's Vision

Question: *Where is love going to take us? I know we're following Jesus, but what lies ahead?* Quite frankly, the future is unseen. As we devote our lives to this thing called love, we don't really know what to expect. We need a vision. Where do you want love to take you? What changes do you want to see take place in you and in those around you? Before we answer this, we have to take a look back at where we came from.

Our culture is sick. It's dirty. It's deadly, and we live in it. We've found our defense. It's Jesus. He's given us the living water so that we may be in the world and not of it. We know not to take the poison. But what about the others who are taking this poison daily and dying from it? It's a slow death, but it spreads like fire. We have an epidemic on hand. We have to do something about this. Love. We know that love is the answer, but how exactly is this going to make a difference? *I know love is my weapon, but what's the plan?* We need a strategy.

So now it's your turn. You're in charge of developing a strategy. You've got a weapon that you can use every moment of the day. Now you've got to decide how you're gonna use it. We need a vision. I can't give you a vision. This is between you and God. This is you saying, *God, reveal to me Your plan for how You desire to use me.* God is calling you. He is calling you right now. He has a place He wants to use you right now. Don't look to tomorrow because God's not there yet. He wants to use you in every moment. His plan was for you to read this book. He is preparing you for something. So in the end, what do you need to do? Be open and eager to hear from God. Listen for His call. Look for the opportunity He is giving you. Vision: how is God going to use me? Once He gives it to you, run with it. Our goal is to love all people, so that the broken may see Christ in us and turn to Him in repentance and faith. God may give you some crazy ideas on how to live this love. Do what He says. God asks people to do crazy things. If He asks you, don't hesitate to obey Him. Love is easier when we have a vision for how God's going to use us.

Expect change. It might only be in you, or it might be in others, but it will surely take place. Look forward to the change. Set goals for the changes you want to see. Love will see these things accomplished for the glory of God. Your heart longs for it. Let your heart give you a vision. Let your heart paint a picture of love in action, of the battlefield, and victory of love. Culture stands no chance against love. Dwell on the aftermath of the love bomb that God is about to drop from Heaven on this society. This is your fight. This is our victory. This is God's glory.

Dare To Dream

Our world has problems. Through experience with our own problems, we've learned that Christ is the solution. The love He displayed for us is the answer. So we've taken this love upon ourselves. We're carrying it to the world. The sad thing is we can get disheartened rather quickly. The world's problems are bad. Some of them seem fixable but many seem impossible to solve. I'm inviting you to dream with me. No, I'm daring you to say, *I can't solve these problems. Nobody can solve them. But my God is the God of the impossible. He will give me strength to accomplish what I can't do. Through love, the impossible will be accomplished. Christ will make the difference.* I believe

God is going to throw some problems your way. Maybe they will be possible, but I have a feeling God's gonna reveal some impossible problems with the world. When God does this, He's saying, *You see this? This isn't right. Now, do something about it.* At first, He's not going to show you how to fix the problem. He will simply call you to fix it. What's He gonna call you to? Keep your eyes open for the impossible problems. If you're in love, God's gonna use you to solve these problems.

It's like we're taking a test. We come across a problem, we know the answer, but we don't know how to mark the answer. The fact that we know the answer isn't going to matter unless we know how to mark it. It's that simple. We already know the answer is love. But that doesn't matter if we don't know how to physically implement it. It's like the answer bubbles are invisible. We want to fill them in but we can't. We are thinking, *How on earth am I supposed to do this? This is impossible.* We get frustrated because we can't see how the answer, love, is supposed to fit in. Therefore, we give up because the problem is impossible. On our own, this is true. We'll never figure it out. But God wants to help us. He knows how it all fits together. He knows how to use love to make the difference. But God's not gonna make us figure it out on our own. He wants to guide our every step.

The first step is most important. We have to submit to Him. That's why I'm daring you to dream. You have to be a dreamer to think the world's problems can be solved by love. Dream. Say, *I believe God can do the impossible through me.* Dreaming isn't enough though. We need to follow where Jesus leads us. We need confidence, devotion, and obedience to God if we want to see our dreams become reality. If we obey, they will.

120 Love Is Here: A Teenager's Call to (Outstretched) Arms

Part Six: **THE PLAN**

Love Is Here: A Teenager's Call to (Outstretched) Arms

XVI. Locating The Threat

In the last chapter, we looked at the big picture. We took a look at the problems in our world, and we learned that God is calling us to bring the solution to those problems through love. I told you that I don't have all the answers. I'm not that smart. I'm just a normal teenager. Nevertheless, I want to eliminate one problem. I don't want any of us to be able to claim ignorance on this issue anymore. To put it plain and simple, relationships take the place of Christ in the lives of teenagers.

Relationships are a threat to all of us because we all have them. We need to locate those relationships that are possible threats, and use love to protect ourselves and others from the deadly satisfaction they can offer. You may be saying, *Woah! Satisfaction? Deadly? I don't think I agree with that.* All I'm saying is that the living water is all that we need, and when we turn to Christ and not people for this satisfaction, the relationships themselves become more satisfying. I know it sounds confusing. The idea is that when Christ is filling you up, you can live those relationships better than ever before because Christ is in control.

Close Relationships Are Targets

I'm about to make a rather obvious point: The friends that you aren't close to aren't a threat. Please, don't get ahead of me. This doesn't justify disconnecting yourself from every relationship. That would be a bad idea. God has placed people close to us for a reason. Oh, and by the way, the reason is not so they can satisfy your spiritual needs. Here's where things get messy.

We know that God has placed people close to us for a reason. Yet, we also can assume that the close relationships are the ones that we are most likely to place above Christ. Where does that leave us? Well, not at peace. That's for sure. We have to keep a watchful eye. We can't let our guard down. If we're truly focused on Christ all the time, it won't be an issue. Unfortunately, we are going to get distracted. It's inevitable. But the key thing is being watchful. The sooner we refocus on Christ the better. In our close relationships, we need to consistently reevaluate our focus. We must commit to this. It should become a habit. Close relationships are beneficial, but only when our focus is on Christ.

Special Scrutiny Of The Opposite Sex

The world would like to tell us, teenagers, that we need romantic relationships, that we need a special companion of the opposite sex. It's obvious that the world wants us to believe that. The media points to it.

Our entire culture points to it. Sometimes we encourage it without realizing. You may already know this, but the world is lying.

The world is trying to trick us. Honestly, I think it's pretty easy for us to notice this lie and make our decisions regardless of what the world says. That's good. That's what we *should* be doing. We know it's stupid to give in to peer pressure and all that. But that's not what worries me. Saying *no* to the world and *yes* to God gets easier the more you do it. So I'm thinking the problem comes when we're on a roll of saying *yes* to God and *no* to the world.

At this point, we've devoted ourselves to love. We're trying to reflect Christ to those with whom we have close relationships. So what I'm saying is it's easy to get distracted by the opposite sex. That's the truth. I would say that the opposite sex is the biggest, or one of the biggest, distractions on our walk with Christ. Why? Because they complete us. They have the other brand of heart. The one we lack. I've said it before. We need this other half in our lives. The fact is, spiritually, we don't need it from the opposite sex. God offers it as well. He has both a male and female heart. The opposite sex isn't offering the living water. We will grow thirsty again if we're drinking from the opposite sex. *But Zach, you said we need the opposite sex in our lives for the right balance.* Yes, I'm not suggesting you tell the opposite sex, *We can't be friends anymore.* We simply need to keep a close watch on those close relationships with the opposite sex, because it is our tendency to drink from them simply for balance. The balance is still in effect through these relationships even when we are not drinking from them.

Questions

The following is a list of questions to help you detect possible relationship threats. This might seem silly but sometimes we simply need to ask ourselves, *Am I going to anyone before Christ for satisfaction?* So think of a particular relationship with the opposite sex, if applicable, and answer honestly.

Do you think more about God or this person?

Do you spend more time with God or this person?

Do you spend more time in God's word or on this person's Facebook page?

Are you more concerned with how God feels or how this person feels?

Are you more concerned with what God would say about your behavior or what this person would say?

Do you start your day with God or this person?

Do you end your day with God or this person?

If you can't think of someone or you want a larger perspective, you can replace *this person* with *someone else* in the questions above. I hope that you were honest with yourself. If you weren't, go back and do it again.

Questions Explained

I know what you're thinking, *Wow, just when I thought Zach couldn't get any lamer, he comes up with these ridiculous questions. I already know all the right answers*. I'm proud of you for knowing the right answers. But let me ask you, if God were looking at your answers, what would He say? Is there someone stealing us from our best friend? Are we ditching Jesus because we think someone else is better for us? God deserves way more than we could ever give Him. In fact, you'd have to live a sinless life and be executed for a crime you didn't commit in order to save the criminal's life if you wanted to satisfy God. Unfortunately, we've all sinned, and therefore we fall short of His glory (Romans 3:23). We need to give God all that we have.

People have the ability to steal from us. They can steal our time, our thoughts, our passion, our everything. I say *steal*, but we really give it to them willingly. Why? Because it makes us feel good for a moment. By giving everything we have to people, we are stealing from God. You wouldn't steal from your best friend, so why would we steal from God?

I wanted you to answer those questions because we need to notice when we are stealing from God. We need to notice it, and we need to stop it. We need to quit giving ourselves to people, especially the opposite sex. We need to give back to God. He deserves more than we could ever give, but our sacrifice, His love through us, is a "pleasing aroma" to Him (Ephesians 5:2). Close relationships with the opposite sex don't need to steal us from God. These relationships can provide a balance in our lives. They can be beneficial, but we need to give to God like He is actually our best friend. He wants to be your actual best friend. He is a faithful friend. Let's give ourselves to Him.

XVII. Taking The First Step...In The Opposite Direction

We've located the threat. God has made us aware of the relationships in our lives that are stealing from Him. So what's the next step? We have to eliminate the threat. I'm not saying you should pray to God and ask Him to take this person out of your life. I also don't support you taking "eliminating the threat" into your own hands, if you know what I mean. You see, God can change us, but we can't change other people. We can't say, *Oh, God's will is for this person to get out of my life.* We have to be eager to work through it. We especially have to be eager when dealing with fellow Christians. My point is: Don't give up on the relationship. God can turn it into something pleasing to Him. *So what do I have to do? What is my part in fixing the relationship?* Good question.

Draw Near To Him, and He Will Draw Near To You

This is a phrase I'm tempted to repeat over and over again: "Draw near to God, and He will draw near to you" (James 4:8 NASB). We need to take a step back from these relationships. We need to give ourselves a time out. It's not a punishment though. It's like taking a vacation. Time alone with God is paradise. So get back to the basics. Take a break from all the craziness of friends and social life. Go home. Relax with God. In this way, we can experience the difference between going to people to be filled and allowing ourselves to be filled by God alone. I don't have a blueprint for what this all looks like. But I have a feeling that taking a step towards God will result in a step out of the relationship. This is okay. We need the timeout/vacation more than ever. It's through drawing near to Christ that we realize the truth that He is all we need.

Make Your Decision Clear, Do Not Waver

Compromise. It's saying, *I want to be faithful to the promise I've made, but I'm gonna need to bend the rules in this particular situation.* Compromise is the opposite of integrity. When we stand firm by our convictions and reject compromise, we are living with integrity. This is something we need if we are to truly seek God. It's easy to return to those relationships when we think we are so filled up on the living water, we won't be tempted by that relationship anymore. It's easy to think that we can drink from both God and people. But we can't. We've decided to put God first, and we're gonna do that with integrity. We can't be on the fence over who we're gonna put first. The decision needs to be made clear. Integrity v. Compromise is the struggle inside of us, but we have a struggle outside too.

People are gonna wonder what's wrong with us. They're gonna ask why we're being so "anti-social". *Why do they have to?* They shouldn't have to. If they knew we were all about putting Jesus first from the start, they wouldn't have to wonder. The world doesn't like being placed under Jesus. It doesn't like when we choose Jesus over friends (I Peter 4:4). The world hates us when we do that. I'm asking you right now to make it clear to the world by what you proclaim through the way that you live. Make it loud and clear. Make it heard that Jesus is your best friend, that He is Lord of your life and first above all.

Come To An Understanding

Get your story straight. The reason you stepped out of that relationship was because you had previously been looking to the world for satisfaction, and now you're looking to God. This is what you tell people. This is what people need to know, not a bunch of gossip. This is being serious about relationships. This is being serious about love. Through it all, we point people to Jesus. We reflect Him to everyone. Remember, you can't change the other person in that relationship, but you can reflect Christ by the way you handle it.

Delight In The Lord

Maybe you feel overwhelmed by some of the things I've been saying. If that's you, just remember that our goal is for our relationships to be pleasing to the Lord. We desire to honor Him. We desire to bring glory to His name. We desire to lift Him up above all. If you understand that and you strive to do it daily, that's all you can do. Our relationship with Jesus Christ is the basis for loving people in our earthly relationships. Success in

God's eyes isn't determined by what others think of you but by your joyful obedience to Him. Above all else, we have to listen to God and do what He says because we seek to give Him all the glory and honor and praise (I Peter 1:7).

My words are only advice. God's words are commands. We are His servants. We seek to be found good and faithful in the end. That's why we delight in His presence. That's why we get excited about worship. We love God. But He loves us more than we could ever love Him. He wants to protect you. He wants to give you shelter. God wants to help you through whatever you're going through. But you have to talk to Him. You have to give Him your undivided attention. That's why it's a big deal if we're being distracted by relationships. Your most intimate relationship will be the solution to your problem by default. But if it's not God, the solution is going to fail big-time. That's why we delight in the Lord when He is our most intimate relationship. He satisfies. You who thirst will thirst no more.

XVIII. Brothers And Sisters

In this final chapter, I want to let you in on a little secret. What I'm about to tell you is sometimes hard to understand, and if we do understand it, it's even harder to do anything with it. There's a phrase that the Church uses all the time. Some use it more than others. I believe it's becoming less popular. It's been around since the time of Christ. In fact, Jesus was the one who came up with the idea. I've been using this phrase quite a bit. So what is it? Brothers and sisters. You're saying, *What's so secretive about that?* The meaning behind the phrase, "brothers and sisters", is life-changing. So what does it mean? *Well, that's a stupid question. We all know what it means already. You must be crazy to think that one phrase is life-changing.* Well, I am crazy, and it is life-changing. Let me unpack it for you.

Christians Of The Opposite Sex Are Family

Think of the Christians you know. Think of how those friends are different from your others. Maybe you notice something, maybe you don't. Our relationships with Christians are entirely different from other relationships. It's important to remember that the only relationship that will follow us into eternity is that of Christian brothers and sisters, not your family, not your friends, not your spouse, not your kids. Those are earth-bound and have no place in eternity. Fellowship, on the other hand, is divine. We are true family because Christ has brought us together. Anything outside of fellowship is worthless in comparison. I'm not saying relationships with those that don't know Christ are pointless. We need those relationships too. We're supposed to reach the unreached. But we must remember that those relationships only have worth when we are doing our job of introducing them to our Savior. The ideal end result is another Christian brother or sister.

My point is that the relationships we have inside of fellowship are heavenly. They are transcendental. They will exist in eternity. None other will. So let me ask you, do you value those relationships with your true brothers and sisters? If they exist in Heaven, they should have ultimate value. Do I need to say it again? Fellowship, God-honoring relationships with other Christians, is heavenly.

If you happen to be a single child of God, let me tell you something: you have the opportunity to taste Heaven. Our society tells us being single isn't worth it. I'm telling you to treasure your taste of Heaven. If you get married, you'll leave your family. Relationships will change. Unfortunately, when dealing with marriage and couples, you can't treat everyone the same. Your first priority becomes your family, not your Christian friends (I Corinthians 7:33-34). Why waste this time? It would be stupid to hate being single. When you die, you're gonna be single, and it's going to be perfect. Why settle for less? Single is the closest to Heaven you'll be until you die. We need to spend this time with our true family, without the distractions our culture throws at us (I Corinthians 7:29-31).

I'm passionate about this because I believe it's the key we've been missing. The opposite sex is already your true family in Christ. You can't get any closer than that. We need to remind ourselves of this especially when we're around those we're attracted to. I mean literally attracted. You should know who I'm referring to. Even so, it goes for all of our relationships. This is as good as it gets until we die. Don't trade God's gift of singleness for something worthless. There's a time for everything. This is the time to be single and love it. We are family today, tomorrow, and through all of eternity.

We Are All Partners In The Faith

I know you're probably sick of me talking about being single. I won't talk about it anymore. I want to bring up the idea of being alone. I'm sure we've all felt alone at some point. I'm not gonna say, *Well, you're never alone if you're a child of God. Jesus is always with you.* It's true that He's with us. He made that promise long ago. But I think some of us are trying to live love on our own. You don't have to. We are meant to go through this life with our brothers and sisters (II Timothy 2:22). Not only are we supposed to walk alongside each other, but we're also supposed to help each other stay focused. We're partners. Each of us has to do our part to help our brothers and sisters. We are not meant to be alone in this. The purpose of life is to love. The purpose of our brothers and sisters is to help catalyze and sustain love. Our faith is what connects us, but too often it's missing. We have a mission. We have to stop fooling around. We need to hold each other accountable to love. We're in a war. This is our army. We don't goof off in war. Christ's Kingdom is advancing but we find ourselves retreating. Let's get back in it. Let's fight alongside our brothers and sisters as partners in love.

Close Friendships Do Not Mean Better Friendships

I want to reiterate a point I made earlier. Our close friendships aren't necessarily better than those less close. I believe that we influence everyone we come in contact with. I just want to ask you to look for how God is using your "less important" relationships. I know none of our relationships are on the same level, but I think we should value them all. Don't just love the people you're closest to. Love everybody. It's easy to say. It's hard to accomplish. It's something we should work at. All interaction we have with people can reflect Christ. Let's make the effort to do that. Especially love all your brothers and sisters for we are one body.

A Shared Faith And Life In Jesus Christ

God created all living things. He made you and me. He designed each of us. He wrote our story long ago. Our lives are simply the stories He has written. We can't change them. He has planned our every breath. He created us to worship Him and praise Him as the one and only God. He loves us passionately. He knows we struggle with sin. So He sent His Son to earth to live a sinless life. Jesus lived without sin. He modeled love to us. Then He was executed on a cross. People thought He was going to set Himself up as King and defeat the Romans. That would have been a good idea. But God had a better idea.

He decided He would make forgiveness of sin available to all. He decided He would send His Son to die on the cross as a sacrifice for our sins. He decided all we would have to do is believe that Jesus accomplished this on the cross and that He came back to life after three days in the grave. He did all this. It was recorded in the Bible by four different people. If we believe, we can experience forgiveness and eternal life. We pray once to Jesus, accept Him as our Savior, and come to life. This starts our journey.

We are on that journey now. Many have been distracted or have never started. The story has turned tragic. People don't believe. The world lies to us. The world tells us our faith is worthless. They say Jesus wasn't God. They say there is no God. They say this life is all there is for us. We have to do something about this. Many of us are only teenagers. But we have the same purpose. Our life is love. Our love is a result of faith in Christ. His Kingdom will come (I Corinthians 15:24). He will return. He will reign forever. But darkness has covered the earth. We need to shine. We are the only light, so we need to shine bright. This is what life's all about. Let's live it like we believe. The power that raised Christ from the grave is alive inside of us (Romans 8:11). Let's fight for the resurrection. Our culture is waiting to destroy us. But we will charge without fear. Our faces set, our battle cry we shout, *Love is here!*

Love Is Here: A Teenager's Call to (Outstretched) Arms

outro: **Practice What You Preach**   June 11, 2010

Thank you for listening to the message God gave me. I began writing this book last summer. It's summer once again, and I'm crossing the finish line of this work. It has been an interesting year. After finishing the first draft last summer, I decided I would live out my message for a year and write this section as a response to my experience and an official conclusion to *Love Is Here*. I completely underestimated how God would work in my heart.

You see, I thought God had done most of the work before I even began writing. He had given me this message in its entirety and allowed me to experience it in my life. I thought that was all I would need to complete this book, but God had other plans.

Without getting into details, I basically faced these relationship issues all over again. God put me to the test. Instead of practicing what I preached in this message, I put it on hold midway through the year. By Christmas, my views on relationships had changed. I still believed I knew how to honor God, but I thought I had found a new way to do so. Instead of keeping an eye on my close relationships, I decided to let them fall into intimacy. I told God that I wanted to be intimate in my love for others as He had been intimate in His love for me. I told Him that I believed this was the pinnacle of love.

The moment I began to live for this belief, I started down the road of destruction. I began to live for *my* love as opposed to *Christ's* love. There were moments of satisfaction, but it didn't last. In the end, only hurt remained. I had produced only mistakes. But God brought me back to this message. He gave me wisdom to learn from my mistakes. This isn't where I will explore God's intimate love in relationships. That's not the message of this book. Nevertheless, I want you to know that God loves you intimately, and He wants an intimate relationship with you. Such a relationship will lead you into a deeper understanding and expression of love that I have not communicated here.

Although I still believe that intimacy can be reflective of Christ and honoring to God, I no longer believe it to be the pinnacle of love. *Love Is Here* only exists because God completed a work in my life. I listened to His voice, and I followed His steps. And I failed in my relationships. I left scars that I can't hope to heal. But I know someone who can. He is why I returned to finish this work. He is Healer. He is my comfort and my hope. He is the Commander of our Army. He is the one who has called you to His Kingdom. He is the road to revolution.

…And He is the reason love is here.

www.ingramcontent.com/pod-product-compliance
Lightning Source LLC
Chambersburg PA
CBHW031400040426
42444CB00005B/360